PRAISE FOR *GROW WITH PURPOSE* AND JOEY BRANNON

"I love Joey Brannon's *Grow with Purpose* because he is helping small business people with the most important parts of their long-term growth—creating values and a purpose for their business. A small business that has its purpose and values clearly identified and communicated is a great company to own and also a great place to work. Joey's *Grow with Purpose* is helping business people think through and put into practice the critical issues of values, vision, mission, and the reason to have a company in the first place."

—Steve Wilson

Founder, Hide-Away Storage

"In my fourteen years of chairing the peer-driven business boards known as C12, I have never met a business owner or CEO who doesn't want to run a company fueled with the enthusiasm of a staff aligned on, and engaged in, a shared mission. Building a great business with a great purpose is in the lexicon of today's top-performing businesses in the marketplace. Kudos, Joey."

—Chuck Frary

Managing Chair, C12

"Joey has been a great asset for this company. He is an integral part of our success. His knowledge and experience has helped us get a handle on growth, put aside the daily urgencies, build a solid foundation, and implement solid processes. Joey's strategic planning guidance has enabled us to move our company forward into the future with great people so we can continue to grow with purpose and fulfill our mission of making an eternal difference in people's lives."

—Gary Curry
Founder, Roofing by Curry

"Joey has been more than a CPA, business strategist, adviser, and confidant - he is a true friend. I suspect most of his clients would say the same because of his extraordinary care in developing relationships. He leads Axiom Strategic in an exemplary manner to clearly demonstrate that he practices what he preaches. Joey has inspired me to be a better leader and to care deeply for my internal and external customers. He asks questions that I need to answer, but may not have considered otherwise, which make me stretch and grow. I appreciate his counsel and his coaching, but even more, his example of integrity and caring friendship. Thank you for honoring me by including our story in yours."

—Dean Burnside
Owner and Operator, Good News Pest Solutions

"I met Joey a couple years ago in a C12 group, which are typically C-level business owners or managers that share best practices in all aspects of business. In our day-long monthly meetings, I saw firsthand his ability to problem solve and analyze situations with clarity and ease. Joey possesses a level of expertise in accounting with practical applications and processes that truly make a difference.

I have been very fortunate in my career of over thirty years to work with business advisors and to know the value of having an outside perspective speak to the decisions I have made. I have been around many successful business people who have paid a high price for their success—usually at the expense of their family. The thing I appreciate most about Joey is the balance he demonstrates and brings with his advice to winning in all areas of your life."

—Skip Stanton
Owner, Aqua Plumbing & Air

GROW *with* PURPOSE

GROW *with* PURPOSE

Building a
MISSION-DRIVEN
BUSINESS

JOEY BRANNON

Published by Advantage, Charleston, South Carolina.
Member of Advantage Media Group.

ADVANTAGE is a registered trademark, and the Advantage colophon is a trademark of Advantage Media Group, Inc.

Printed in the United States of America.

10 9 8 7 6 5 4 3 2 1

ISBN: 978-1-59932-922-2
LCCN: 2019934685

Cover design by Carly Blake.
Layout design by Megan Elger.

This publication is designed to provide accurate and authoritative information in regard to the subject matter covered. It is sold with the understanding that the publisher is not engaged in rendering legal, accounting, or other professional services. If legal advice or other expert assistance is required, the services of a competent professional person should be sought.

Advantage Media Group is proud to be a part of the Tree Neutral® program. Tree Neutral offsets the number of trees consumed in the production and printing of this book by taking proactive steps such as planting trees in direct proportion to the number of trees used to print books. To learn more about Tree Neutral, please visit **www.treeneutral.com**.

TreeNeutral

Advantage Media Group is a publisher of business, self-improvement, and professional development books and online learning. We help entrepreneurs, business leaders, and professionals share their Stories, Passion, and Knowledge to help others Learn & Grow. Do you have a manuscript or book idea that you would like us to consider for publishing? Please visit **advantagefamily.com** or call **1.866.775.1696**.

To small business owners striving to build a legacy
greater than just profits.

TABLE OF CONTENTS

Why "Grow with Purpose"?

It All Starts in Your Head

The Message Needs a Messenger

Effective Leadership in a Small Business

Customers Come Second

FOREWORD

Driven. Purposeful. Tenacious. Passionate. Faithful. These are some of the words that come to mind as I think about the man I've known for almost fifteen years. I've had the privilege of calling Joey Brannon my friend, my business coach, a Spartan race warrior, a great husband to his wife, an awesome father to his three children, and a genuine Christian man.

When Joey first mentioned he was writing a book on business, I couldn't wait to see what he produced. What you're about to read is a play-by-play manual for a business just starting out or one that has been around for years, but never truly found its moorings. It's easy to start a business—almost 630,000 of them begin every year! Over 50 percent of those same businesses flame out in the first four years mostly due to incompetence and lack of experience.

What makes Joey Brannon stand out in the crowd is not only his bald head and CrossFit fanaticism, but also his business acumen and purposeful living. I've watched him work with clients with business revenues in the multimillions and quickly assess what ails them. Some of them aren't that broken, but Joey's skills allow him to see the story behind the numbers and, with great precision, he masterfully shares how to get from here to there.

We've spent hundreds of hours together talking about our common love of family, faith, business, and baseball—in that order! You'll find within this book not only the ingredients of making a good business great, but also the key to purposeful living which I've witnessed in Joey and in the businesses he works with. Through personal stories, he shares the true measure of a great business—the ability to unselfishly care for those around you, in your community, and around the world.

It's rare to find a business book that contains the nuts and bolts of building a great business along with helping you define a purpose greater than your paycheck. Get ready to enjoy *Grow with Purpose*.

—**Doug Poll, CPLC**
C12 Group Chair, Southwest Florida

ACKNOWLEDGMENTS

I am lucky to have more than a few heroes in my life. Not the kind you find in comic books or movies, but real, live human beings who have shown me that extraordinary things are possible by ordinary people. I have been blessed to work for and alongside many of them as the founder of Axiom, a consulting practice that serves this special group.

These are men and women who own small businesses that are accomplishing great things. Their companies are literally changing the world through the business they carry out in the marketplace. Small business owners are some of the most altruistic and generous people you will ever meet. They create opportunities for employees. They meet the unspoken needs of their customers. They give second chances and become extended families. They invest in their communities through time, money, and services without expecting anything back in return. They see their role as one of steward and mentor.

Pretty much everything I've learned and share here I have learned from these giants, these heroes who have blessed me with their time and wisdom. We have done some amazing things together and it brings great joy to see them reaching their visions and accomplishing great good in the world. Without them, nothing you read in the pages that follow would have been written.

There is another group that deserves special attention. They are the families of those same business owners, and I count my family among them.

The spouse of a small business owner possesses extraordinary qualities of patience, encouragement, risk tolerance, wisdom, discernment, forgiveness, compassion, and perseverance. My wife, Josie, has been my model for these traits. Every small business owner in the world will tell you that what happens at the office is, in large measure, dependent on what is happening at home. Work holds little reward or lasting legacy if the fruits of achievement are not born out in the family that made them possible. I may take many things for granted, but the role of my family, and especially my wife, is not one of them. I owe them everything, both what has passed to this date and what is to come in the future. I would not want it any other way.

The last group of heroes is the small cadre of friends I count as professional colleagues. They are other firm owners and consultants with whom I share war stories, new insights and life lessons in equal measure. It can be lonely as a firm owner, but I am fortunate to be able to count my own parents among this esteemed group.

Also included are those, too numerous to name one-by-one, who have joined me in The Consulting CPA program. These men and women are changing the face of the public accounting profession by enabling small business owners to expand and deepen their mission using practical tools and a common-sense approach to strategic planning and execution. They have trusted me with the growth of their own firms and by extension with the success of their clients. I value each and every one of you beyond the words I can express here. This book is one more effort to express my thanks and tireless commitment to give you something of enduring value.

ABOUT THE AUTHOR

Joey Brannon is the founder of Axiom Strategic Consulting. Over the course of the last twenty years, he has worked with hundreds of business owners. During that time, he has worked on accounting systems, tax return preparation and planning, financial forensics, international compliance, ERP systems, and management issues. Through constant study and over twenty years of experience, he has learned what works and what doesn't work for small business owners. Today, his firm helps small business companies between $2 million and $30 million in revenue build and execute strategic plans for growth. He works with the business owners, their families, and their leadership teams to work through the principles in this book.

In 2016, Joey launched The Consulting CPA, a program to teach other CPAs how to build strategic consulting into their existing tax and accounting practices. Since its initial launch, The Consulting CPA has trained dozens of CPAs in the US and chartered accountants internationally in the structure and execution of strategic planning and execution for small businesses.

Joey is a native of Florida and lives with his wife, Josie, and their three children in southwest Florida.

Why "Grow with Purpose"?

I grew up saying I would never be a CPA. My dad was a CPA and he worked crazy hours. Me, I wanted to be a scientist, but it turned out that one of my earliest life lessons was "never say never," because after graduating school I joined my dad's firm. There, I spent a ridiculous amount of time with small business owners. I took it for granted at the time, but it was actually a great opportunity. Very few twenty-somethings enjoyed the kind of access I had to small business owners two and three times my age, and even fewer were given the chance to screw things up as badly I could. My dad was incredibly trusting. It helped that I inherited his work ethic, and whatever problems I created, I got the "opportunity" to solve. Small business owners, I discovered, were accustomed to screwups. Their whole world consisted of screwups and uncertainty and judgment calls and stuff you couldn't see in the financial statements. I was hooked. Those four years with my dad would shape everything that came after.

My great joy, besides my faith and family, is working alongside small business owners. It is a joy I first discovered working with my dad's clients. Over time, it led me to

Small business owners, I discovered, were accustomed to screwups. Their whole world consisted of screwups and uncertainty and judgment calls and stuff you couldn't see in the financial statements. I was hooked.

work with a group of serial entrepreneurs and start-ups, a couple of accounting firms, and hundreds of clients. Eventually that same joy led me to start my own CPA firm, and later to sell the firm so that I could spend less time on tax returns and more time helping owners and their teams grow the business. Axiom Strategic Consulting was born out of our work with small businesses, usually with $2 million to $30 million in revenue. This book is written with small business owners in mind, and it outlines much of what we do with clients. In its pages, you will read stories of real clients with real problems, just like yours. Where the stories are good, I have proudly championed our clients by name. Where bad, I have come up with pseudonyms.

As a group, small business owners are some of the most generous and caring people you will ever met. Those who don't care usually don't stay in business very long. Those who prosper are the ones who learn to identify needs around them and meet those needs while turning a profit.

But not all businesses are equal. Some are very successful while most just survive and a lot struggle. What makes the difference?

Successful businesses have their house in order. Order is a big part of success, and we will cover that. But there is success and then there is SUCCESS. And I am not talking about dollars. SUCCESS-

FUL businesses are those on a mission. They see what they do as playing a bigger part than just generating profits. In short, SUCCESSFUL businesses grow with purpose.

This book is divided into three parts. Part One is about finding purpose. Almost every business starts with grand ambition but eventually loses its way. We are going to start from the beginning and build (or rebuild) the foundation for solid, purposeful growth.

Part Two is about getting our house in order. All the purpose in the world will not help a terrible businessperson. Small business owners need to get the basics right, from processes and procedures to knowing and understanding their financials.

Part Three is about the two keys to executing growth. After having built the foundation and put the house in order, we must direct the time, attention, and energy of our leaders, and we must do it from a posture of service. This is what separates success from SUCCESS.

You can gain valuable insight from any of the parts and any of the chapters within the parts. But I firmly believe, and indeed have seen in my daily work with small business clients, that it takes all three to build a mission-driven business—a business that can truly make a difference in the world. And that is what I and the team at Axiom are about. We want to make a difference, one small business at a time. Let's get started with yours.

Part One

FINDING PURPOSE

CHAPTER ONE

It All Starts in Your Head

Dean is the second owner of a nearly thirty-year-old pest control company. He bought the business from the original founder after working there for a number of years. Over the course of ten years or so, Dean quadrupled the size of his company. He invested in a management team and was able to hand off daily responsibilities like accounting, sales, operations, and customer service. Over time, Dean had done something very few small business owners are able to accomplish—he had joined the rarified air of multimillion-dollar business owners. It was about this time that Dean and I went to a Baltimore Orioles spring training game together.

Dean and I had known each other for a while, and during that baseball game I challenged his vision for the business. (It's what I often do in my line of work. As a second-generation CPA, I grew up out of the world of CPAs and tax returns and found my fulfillment in helping small business owners grow their business.) Under

Deans' leadership, the pest control company's growth had taken off, but then it plateaued. I felt like the only reason sales had stopped growing was that Dean had become comfortable … too comfortable. He had bought the company with a determination to grow it to $2 million in revenue and twenty employees, and that had been accomplished. But what next?

Although they had a mission statement on the wall, no one knew where that mission statement was supposed to take them. To use an analogy, Dean had spent considerable time and money tuning up the car, making sure it was ready for a long journey. But the company was simply doing laps around a $2 million track. It was time to pull out a map and get the car back on the open road, with a clear destination and a timeline to create some urgency.

Dean brought me in, and we started pushing him and his team to think more clearly about where they wanted to take their business. We began to work very deliberately on four areas that would become the foundation for future growth: values, vision, why, and mission.

Your VVWM Core

If you are like most business owners, you started out with a very clear sense of purpose and direction. You spent years working for someone else and thinking of all the ways you would do it better if it were your company. Eventually it became your company, and all those decisions became yours to make. But as the days turned into months and years, a laundry list of daily problems and pressing priorities crowded out the dreams you had for your business. Maybe, like Dean, you accomplished a certain level of growth and then plateaued, or maybe you've struggled to grow and achieve the goals you originally set. Whatever the case, at some point you hit an invisible barrier, and today, as you read this, you are no longer content to just let things continue as they have been.

You are in the right place. And the very first order of business is understanding that growth and impact beyond your current experience is dependent on your ability to harness the talents and abilities of a team. And you can't recruit, inspire, motivate, direct, redirect, and lead a team if you can't communicate what you are about or your ultimate vision

Whatever the case, at some point you hit an invisible barrier, and today, as you read this, you are no longer content to just let things continue as they have been.

for where you want the team to go. Maybe you have the team in place, maybe you need to go out and recruit them, or maybe you need to get your house in order so that you have the money to go recruiting in the first place. It doesn't matter where you are starting from; you must have something worthwhile to say as the leader of your company to interest people in signing up and helping you accomplish your grand vision for changing the world. Establishing the four pillars of values, vision, why, and mission is the first step.

VALUES

Values persist, no matter what line of business you are in, because they are a reflection of leadership and, in long-standing companies, institutional history. They may even outlive one leader's tenure and become part of the legacy that endures under future leaders. When Collis P. Huntington decided to start Chesapeake Dry Dock and Construction Company in 1886, he held one value above all others: quality. He was willing to make many sacrifices when it came to his contracts to build ships, but quality was not one of them. He is famously quoted as saying, "We shall build good ships here, at a profit if we can, at a loss if we must, but always good ships." Over 130 years later, his company has built more than eight hundred ships. It is the sole supplier of nuclear-class aircraft carriers to the US government and is one of only two companies supplying submarines to the US Navy. Today the company is better known as Newport News Shipbuilding, but the singular value of uncompromising quality that Huntington instilled lives on to this day.

Values are intensely practical. When values become part of the company's reputation, they help recruit the best people. When values are referred to often, they become a compass when making tough decisions. And if values are placed front and center in good times and bad, they serve as ballast when tough times rock the corporate ship.

To understand your own cultural values, start with the process of identifying four to five words that best describe your culture. But it is not just your opinion that counts. Ask your leadership team, veteran employees, new employees, customers, vendors, and friends and family. You might hear words like professional, innovative, integrity, caring, learning, workmanship, opportunity, and fun, but don't just stop at the good stuff. Encourage people to be honest. Find some "secret shoppers" to ask the question for you, and you might also hear words like selfish, opportunistic, and greedy. Rather than shy away from reality, embrace it. Your heart is probably in the right place, but if your actions don't line up with your intentions, you need to hear the truth.

For Dean's company, Good News Pest Solutions, honoring their values included making the game-changing decision that they were only going to use green, sustainable products in their business. When your core product is chemicals that kill things, that's a big deal. By moving away from poisonous chemicals and only working with green products, they did something that was completely in line with their stated values of honesty, integrity, caring, diligence, and fun. At the time, it seemed like a big risk. No one knew if the green products would be as effective as the more toxic chemicals they were replacing. But the community and, ultimately, the industry responded and followed their lead. Being true to their values made Good News a pioneer in the industry and resulted in Dean being pursued as a speaker at trade events and industry conferences to share his story.

VISION

Values persist no matter what goods or services your company is selling. They are a reflection of leadership and culture. Vision is different. It is intensely specific to where your business is going. Good News Pest Solutions' vision is to become a top one hundred pest control company in the United States. That vision is totally unambiguous. It clearly communicates what Dean wants to accomplish. A good vision means the picture in Dean's head is the same picture his employees, customers, and affiliates see.

There is a tendency for no-nonsense, cynical business owners to stand back and say, "All that vision crap sounds good in a book, but I've got real work to do." But good vision is intensely practical. If your work relies on other people helping you get there, you must have a worthy vision. It makes growth possible in several ways.

If your work relies on other people helping you get there, you must have a worthy vision. It makes growth possible in several ways.

First, a good vision shortcuts how you communicate to everyone on your team what you are about and what you are trying to accomplish. Dean's goal is to become a top one hundred company in the industry—not to innovate new products, not to buy up smaller players, not to go paperless, not to build a national brand, not to have a state-of-the-art facility. Good News may do one or more of those things, but they will be done IN SERVICE OF the vision to become a top one hundred company. Everyone knows that whatever priorities or initiatives are launched, they are all done in light of the vision to become a top one hundred company.

Second, a good vision is one of the best recruiting and retention tools you have. The best people want to join a winning team that knows where it is going. If employees know your vision, they can judge for themselves what opportunities might lie ahead. When a worthy vision is communicated often, in as many ways as possible, everyone knows what the boss is about. Plans for the future are not secreted in some innermost circle around the business owner. A good vision turns team members into disciples who can share it with family members, friends, customers, vendors, and anyone else who will listen. A worthy vision gives vendors and suppliers the assurance that your success equals their success.

Finally, a good vision is a litmus test. It can tell you whether you are making decisions that pull you away from it or push you toward it. A vision ensures that goals and priorities are focused in a direction that will actually make a difference over the months ahead, and will tell you what kinds of customers you need to look for and which customers on your current list need to be handed over to your competitors.

To be sure, a vision is an incredibly powerful tool for the small business owner. You can take two businesses that appear to be identical. They sit right across the street from one another. They sell the same product, at the same price, to the same market in essentially the same way. In fact, the only difference between them is that one business owner has a vision to become the next Sam Walton (founder of Walmart) and the other just wants an extra day off per week to go fishing with his granddaughter. To the outside observer, the two businesses appear identical, but down the road they will look vastly different. We may not see it for the next ten or twenty or thirty years, but your vision today is what will determine where you wind up in the future.

Good News Pest Solutions has a vision to become a top one hundred company in their industry—but why did they embrace that particular vision?

WHY?

Simon Sinek popularized the concept of "Start with Why" in his bestselling book of the same name. When someone describes a vision, it's human nature to be curious about what motivates that vision. Answering the question "why?" gives people a window into what makes the company tick. When your "why" resonates with people, they will sign up for what you believe in and become fully engaged. It doesn't matter whether they are employees, customers, vendors, investors, or volunteers. Why makes a big difference.

Our why is literally our values in action.

If you asked Dean, "Why do you want to become a top one hundred company?" he would tell you that when they reach that level they will have the team and resources to employ a full-time "Care Team" for their employees, customers, vendors,

Our why is literally our values in action.

13

and anyone else impacted by the business. Further, they will have a platform for their faith and ministry that the pest control industry will stand up and notice. In short, becoming a top one hundred company represents an expansion of Good News Pest Solution's ministry that is energizing, exciting, and motivating, both to Dean and to everyone who signs up to join him on this journey.

I love having "why" conversations with small business owners. Gary, another client, has endured an incredible string of personal and business hardships—some would even say injustices. He is known for his intense loyalty, giving employees and suppliers not just second chances but tenth, eleventh, and twelfth chances. When you talk to Gary about his why, you hear immense gratitude toward a few individuals who made a big difference at some key moments in his life. He will always give grace and a second chance, even at great personal cost, because he believes second chances have the potential to change lives. With over 150 employees, Gary's second chances have changed a lot of lives.

But not all whys are created equal. If Dean wanted to become a top one hundred company just to line his own pockets, that's not very inspiring to anyone but Dean. Your people need inspiration, and your why holds the power to move them in powerful ways. Sinek believes, and I agree with him, that your why is a powerful tool for inspiring action, not just among your team but also among your customers, suppliers and vendors, family members, and prospects. Sharing your why means baring your soul. It entails vulnerability. But vulnerability, hard as it is, leads to trust, and trust is the stuff that loyal customers, employees, and business partners are looking for.

Sharing your why means baring your soul.

Speaking of vulnerability, let's take a look at my own why as an example. My firm, Axiom Strategic Consulting, is dedicated to helping small businesses grow and is itself a small business. I have a vision to grow Axiom to a string of offices located in major metro areas around the United States. Why? Because I believe that small business done right have a greater impact for good and positive change than any other institution: greater than any church, nonprofit, government program, or charity. Growing Axiom comes out of my natural desire to see more businesses take up that challenge to change the world through positive, intentional, and worthy growth. My point here is that if I am bold enough to share not just my vision, but *why* my vision is important to me, like-minded business owners, consultants, partners, and prospects will line up outside my door. We think alike, and they want to do business with like-minded people.

Growing Axiom comes out of my natural desire to see more businesses take up that challenge to change the world through positive, intentional, and worthy growth.

MISSION

There's a lot of hand wringing over writing mission statements. If you google "How to write a mission statement," you'll get all kinds of dubious advice. There is a reason I address it last with my clients, after we have already covered values, vision, and why. Mission is nothing more than describing what you do and how the world is better off because of it. It's that simple. But simple does not equal easy. You have to do the homework of values, vision, and why first.

Your values describe your culture. They will be most evident to the people who come to work beside you every day, but occasionally a customer or some other outside party will come into contact with your business and experience your values in action.

Your vision describes the thing you are after and why you need everyone's help to get there. Like values, vision is primarily for those on your team, although occasionally it may inspire those who buy from you or who sell to you.

Your why describes your motivations, what makes you tick. Your why can be built into every message, product, and service. It affects marketing, product development, advertising, sales presentations, employee onboarding, training … everything.

As you go through the hard work to develop your values, vision, and why, you should think of it primarily as in investment in your team and your responsibility to them as their leader.

But your mission statement is a little different. Yes, you want your team to know it, but if they aren't fully vested in your values, vision, and why, don't expect them to get excited about a mission statement. On the other hand, if they are fully engaged in your values, vision, and why, they are probably already living out the mission statement (whether they can recite your carefully crafted words or not). The mission statement isn't for your team so much as it is for those outside your four walls. The world at large doesn't have the time, energy, or interest to digest your values, vision, or why. So, you give them a mission statement. It is your best attempt to explain to the uninitiated what you are about.

The mission statement of Good News Pest Solutions is:

> *The world at large doesn't have the time, energy, or interest to digest your values, vision, or why. So, you give them a mission statement.*

SHARING GOD'S GOOD NEWS WHILE SOLVING PEST PROBLEMS WITH GREEN SOLUTIONS.

There's nothing in there about becoming a top one hundred company. There's nothing about the values of honesty, integrity, caring, diligence, and fun. And there's not a lot (although you get an idea) that tells you the reason Dean wants the business to grow is that it will be a greater platform for ministry. But it does a wonderful job of telling someone who knows nothing else about the company what they do and what sets them apart.

A mission statement describes what the business is doing and how it ripples out into the rest of the world. A mission statement is meant for public consumption, so you should use the clearest and most straightforward, plainest language possible. At Axiom, our mission is "To proclaim Christ in the marketplace by teaching small companies the art and science of growth through planning, execution, stewardship, and leadership." I love mission statements that don't use lots of big words, conjunctions, semicolons, dashes, or nonsensical words. "Aligned," "distinguished," "aspirational," and "authoritatively" are words that should be banned from all mission statements.

VVWM in Action

As Dean reevaluated his foundation for growth, he decided to make another strong shift by changing the company's name. Originally, the company was named Macy's Pest Control after the original founder, and Dean kept the name when he bought the company. But one day Dean was sitting in a meeting with several other business owners when one of them had an epiphany. "Dean, why aren't you the good news company? You are always delivering good news." Dean thought about this for a second. One of the things he had drilled into his salespeople was that whatever the situation, they were always delivering good news. "Good news! We didn't find any termites! You're all set for closing." Or "Good news! We found the termites before you bought the house. The seller is going to cover fumigation." Dean also had a passion for sharing God's Good News with his customers. The suggestion was one he couldn't get out of his mind.

It wasn't that the current company name didn't mean anything. It represented a long history of service and excellence. But Dean felt that they were also missing a tremendous opportunity to communicate important elements of their values, vision, why, and mission in the very name of the company. It didn't take long for Dean to make the decision to rename and rebrand the company. Dean's values, vision, why, and mission had become so tangible, so practical in the everyday running of the company that they ultimately led to a change in the most basic, publicly facing thing in the business—the name of the company.

Today, Dean's company is well on its way to becoming a top one hundred company in the pest control industry, and his values, vision, why, and mission come into play every day. That's the point of having them. You must use them every day in making decisions, building plans, evaluating performance, setting goals, mentoring employees, and communicating to the outside world.

The values, vision, why, and mission of a company are more than just words on a page in a company manual. They should inform both big and small decisions. They should have an impact on both day-to-day business and the long-term history of the company.

CHAPTER TWO

The Message Needs a Messenger

Once values, vision, why, and mission are established, it's important that we become experts at communicating them so that they truly make an impact on our employees, customers, and community. One of my mentors has a son who does this superbly—who is also incredibly humble, so I've disguised his name and industry, but you'll get an idea of how values, vision, why, and mission affect the day-to-day business.

Ken owns a construction company that is changing the lives of orphans on the other side of the world, and he's doing it by building houses in some of the wealthiest neighborhoods in the United States. Ken is a relational person, working best in a team and interacting with other people. He loves working with the thirty or so employees in the home office.

Ken's company, Classic Homes, has well-defined values, a clear vision, a compelling why, and a mission that resonates with team members, customers, and subcontractors. It's Ken's job to constantly communicate those things in the course of running the company. Let's take a look at how that happens and how it makes a difference.

CLASSIC HOMES' VALUES:

Compassion: Every decision affects a real person.

Initiative: Great things will be accomplished by those who act first.

Growth: Every day is a chance to learn from mistakes and get better.

Stewardship: We take care of the material things entrusted to us.

CLASSIC HOMES' VISION:

To build five thousand homes.

CLASSIC HOMES' WHY:

Everyone deserves a roof over their heads, and those who are most helpless among us cannot do it for themselves. Classic Homes takes a good portion of the profits from its business and uses it to build orphanages. They've done the math, and it will take about five thousand homes to build, staff, and maintain ten orphanages. Their employees get extended vacation time to take trips to foreign countries every few years with various churches and youth groups. The churches provide labor, while Classic Homes provides the supervision, building materials, and logistics to complete the work. Ken and his team take the words of James 1:27 to heart: "Pure and genuine religion in the sight of God the Father means caring for orphans and widows in their distress."

CLASSIC HOMES' MISSION:

We build quality homes for a higher purpose.

When you look at Ken's typical day, the company's vision, values, why, and mission show up everywhere. His role is to lead by putting them front and center in everything the company does. Here's Ken's "work" day:

On this Tuesday morning, Ken wakes up and meditates on his company vision during his quiet time. During his morning standup meeting with his team, he talks about the value of compassion and how it should mean that individuals are considered first, regardless of the situation. He shares a short story from the previous day on how an employee in the field, Karen, handled herself in the face of an abusive customer. The customer accused her of incompetence, but Karen was able to turn the situation around, scheduling a special inspection to satisfy the customer and avoiding a two-week delay. After sharing the story, Ken asks Karen's supervisor to check in with her today and see if she needs anything further to help this customer.

Later that morning, Ken has an opportunity to talk about each of the four values during a final new hire interview and asks for examples of where the prospective employee might have seen those values in action while working for other companies. What he hears isn't encouraging. After the interview, Ken talks with the manager who needs the hire, and both agree to interview a few more people before making an offer.

Next, Ken approves a press release that leads with their mission statement. He smiles to himself that he no longer has to write the mission statement into the first paragraph with a red pen. Marketing is catching on.

Ken goes to lunch with his general manager, where they discuss whether the next facility they move into will be sufficient to achieve the company's vision of building five thousand homes. It has taken them fifteen years to reach one thousand, but the pace has accelerated exponentially over the last four years. The growth track looks something like four thousand homes in ten years. It's starting to look like they might need two more moves. Both agree to pull some numbers, and Ken says he'll talk to a friend across the country for some advice on how much space they'll need.

After lunch, he asks his sales manager to meet with a radio station to vet upcoming ad spots and make sure they are consistent with their four main company values. The sales manager says he thinks they are, but that no one has explicitly tried to work the values into the ads. He and Ken have a good discussion on how values should inform and affect what they do even when they can't be explicitly identified in the ad's content. Ken knows he's getting somewhere when the manager says, "So stewardship might affect how we negotiate the total ad spend, but we don't have to necessarily talk about stewardship in the ad."

At the end of the day, Ken stops in the office doorway of one of his customer service representatives and asks her for a "story of the day." She tells him about a customer who received one of the company's thank-you cards on the one-year anniversary of their home purchase. The front of the card is a picture of a completed orphanage with thirty-five smiling kids standing in front of a humble building somewhere across the world. But the card doesn't say anything about the orphans or the orphanage. This customer called and got the whole story. She's now a monthly contributor to the foundation that covers the ongoing costs and staffing of the orphanages.

This is an illustration of how your values, vision, why, and mission can spread throughout your day to become an invaluable part of your business without being stuck on a wall or inside a PowerPoint presentation.

By honing in on their values, vision, why, and mission, everyone at the company has a framework for making decisions. And it is those decisions that make Ken's company what it is. With a different set of values, vision, why, and mission, the company would look different, the employees would act differently, and the customers would respond differently. What is true of Ken's business is true of your business. The values, vision, why, and mission will define who you are, what you do, and why you do it.

Contrast this with the way most companies are run, without any defined values, without a vision, without any compelling reason why, and without a mission that anyone knows. Is it any wonder that most companies struggle with customer service, retention, employee morale, and ultimately profitability?

At the same time, we have to realize that just having values, vision, why, and mission isn't enough. We must actively create opportunities to communicate them. They have to be talked about all the time.

At the same time, we have to realize that just having values, vision, why, and mission isn't enough. We must actively create opportunities to communicate them.

Making Tough Decisions
That Put Values First

There are numerous practical applications of values, vision, why, and mission that show up every day, just as in Ken's case. Without question, they should be used as a filter for daily decisions within your company. You should be asking, "Is this choice consistent with our values? Does it move us in the direction of our vision? Does our attitude and behavior reflect our why? When people see us doing this, will it be obvious that we are all about our mission?"

Ken did not put his VVWM on a shelf and say to his team, "Just get the work done." He used VVWM in every aspect of managing and leading his team. These are tools that can help business owners where they often struggle most—in the nuanced and subjective role of dealing with people. Business owners often have little trouble wrapping their arms around the technical and logistical issues facing the business. But when it comes to people, they can use all the help they can get.

People decisions are rarely based on quantitative feedback. There is no black and white report that says, "Here's what this person is doing that doesn't quite sit well with you." But VVWM can go a long way toward making that subjective, qualitative behavior objectively measurable.

For example, when an employee receives more than their fair share of complaints, both from coworkers and customers, we can better understand the situation by using VVWM. When we dig a little deeper (and have VVWM top of mind), we may see that every single one of those complaints for the last two months has been a blatant disconnect from one particular company value. We don't even have to get into who was right and who was wrong. If the handling of the situation was inconsistent with our values, that is the only thing that matters. You can be right all day long, but if you violate our values in the process, that's not okay.

I hear business owners say this all the time. "It's not WHAT he's doing. Honestly, he's doing his job very well. But it's the WAY he's doing it. I just don't know if we can keep him." This is a business owner who has never taken the time to articulate values. Or if they have, those values never make it out of the three-ring binder and into daily conversation.

Business owners like Ken sound totally different. They say things like "Joanne was putting up some really good numbers in her territory, but we just couldn't let her stay. She was making a habit of throwing her teammates under the bus every time something went wrong. I get it. It's frustrating when other people screw up and create problems that aren't your fault. But if one of our company values is loyalty, we've got to have each other's back."

Getting the Best People

VVWM is also a way to weed through all the candidates for a job in search of those rare A-players. Skills and competency are the minimum requirements for a new hire. But most companies stop their formal interviewing there and leave the final decision to intuition or "gut feel." If we use cultural fit as an explicit indicator, we'll spot things that our "gut" will often miss. When we discuss our VVWM with incoming hires during an interview, we get an entirely different set of responses and reactions, versus basing our judgment solely on their abilities, their experience, and whether they seem like a nice person. We're taking the assessment a step further and building a solid team rather than filling an operational hole with a competent and nice person.

This is something I see with new clients, where they do a lot of homework to verify skills and competency to make sure that the person they're about to hire knows HOW to do the job. But they do almost nothing to assess cultural and mission fitness:

- What is this person's potential for future roles as we move toward our vision?

- Does our why resonate with their personal motivations, values, and beliefs?

- Are they excited by the mission they are expected to show up for and serve with enthusiasm every day?

These are risky questions to ask. It's much easier to wrap up the interview and evaluate the prospect with questions like "So how do you think it went? Were they a good person to talk to? Did they seem energetic? Did they seem like they'd fit in?"

Imagine that during your next new hire interview you asked some of the following questions:

- These are our company values. Take a look at them and tell me, have you ever worked for a company or been a customer of a company that did any of these well? What did that look like?

- Which of these values do you think it would be easiest for you to live out, and which would require the most work?

- You've read our vision statement. That's obviously not where we are now, but as we move toward it, how do you think your role in the company might change? How would you want it to change?

- Is our company vision compelling to you?

- What are the similarities and differences between our why and yours?

- How would you feel sharing our mission statement with a customer? With your parents? With your spouse? What would they say about it? How would you respond?

Also, be aware that as you're evaluating them, they're evaluating you as their prospective employer. It says a lot that your vision, values, why, and mission play a feature role in a new hire interview. In a lot of companies, these interviews can be a throwaway part of an otherwise busy day or just checking the box on someone who has stellar qualifications. The fact that you've taken the time to get their thoughts on the bigger business won't be overlooked by the person you are interviewing. The odds are good that you will pull people into your company's orbit who want more than just a job. The right ones will sit up straighter and realize you are pulling better answers and better thinking out of them than the company that just made them a sweet offer as they were driving to your place for the interview.

Developing the Best People

But talking about VVWM isn't just for new hires. It is also the most effective way to identify those who need to be promoted from within. Before we start working with a new client, I spend a lot of time interviewing different people at all levels in the company. It was during one of these interviews that I met Wilmar, an ambitious young guy pegged as an up-and-comer. Wilmar just needed a little more experience before graduating to a supervisor position.

I asked him, "Let's say that you knew you were starting here tomorrow as a new hire. Knowing everything you know about the company now, what's one thing you would like to change so that you would start off your first day on the right foot?" Others had talked about pay raises and better training programs, but Wilmar said, "I wish we could find a way so that guys would get it from Day 1." I asked him what he meant.

He said, "Look, the owner is incredibly generous and he genuinely wants everybody to succeed here. He always puts himself second or last. People don't realize the opportunity they have here. They don't realize that this company is different from every other company that they're going to have the chance to work for.

"If they could understand the supportive, selfless company they're working for from Day 1, their first impression would be different. Sure, they know what the job expectations are, but if they really got it on Day 1, they would also know what is most important to the owner—that it's really all about them. If that happened, I think we would have better people a year or even two years into the job, because they might carry themselves a little differently."

What is interesting about this story is that Wilmar's company didn't yet have a defined set of values. They didn't have a vision. They didn't have a compelling why. They didn't have a concise mission statement. But they got lucky and Wilmar resonated with everything they were about. He was the cultural equivalent of a round peg in a perfectly fitting round hole.

But what Wilmar was saying—what he was shouting out and somewhat frustrated with—was that he didn't want to leave it up to luck to find the next Wilmar, the next guy who "got it." Without even knowing it, he was screaming for values, a worthy vision, and a mission that would be the most important part of Day 1 on the job.

Wilmar knew instinctively that if we pay more attention to communicating VVWM, we will wind up with better team members—not just because we hire better people, but because we call the people we hire up to greater levels of expectation and achievement.

Growth Requires a Messenger

If we pay more attention to communicating VVWM, we will wind up with better team members—not just because we hire better people, but because we call the people we hire up to greater levels of expectation and achievement.

Chapter One was about crafting the message. This chapter has been about how that message can fuel our growth. One of the first things we have to realize about growth is that there are two kinds. The first kind of growth is internal and personal. We can all improve our businesses by becoming better at our jobs. Owners can sell better to close one more deal, manage time better to get one more project shipped each week, hire better to reduce turnover, and budget better to decrease overhead. But visions that rely only on personal growth are tiny visions.

The second kind of growth requires more than we can do alone. This is the growth required by a worthy vision. In Chapter One, we acknowledged that we can't do it alone. We must leverage the time, talents, and ambitions of people other than ourselves. But the message alone won't do it. The message requires a messenger, someone who will be relentless in talking about values, pointing out examples, and using them to make decisions and quantify qualitative behavior. It requires a messenger who talks about the vision with the team and uses it to set priorities, someone who uses the vision to decide who should be on the team in the first place. It requires a messenger with the courage and confidence to talk about why it all matters. And it requires a messenger who is publicly on mission, not just any mission, but THE mission ... always, without distraction or equivocation or apology.

Are you the messenger your company needs to grow with purpose? Because they won't get it by osmosis. They will not come to your office and ask. They will not pursue you. You must pursue them, and you must do it relentlessly. Your values, vision, why, and mission must infect everything you do before you can expect them to infect everyone around you.

CHAPTER THREE

Effective Leadership in a Small Business

Steve opened his first self-storage facility over forty years ago. Today he has twenty locations and plans to open another twenty within the next ten years. He recently closed a deal that will enable his company to expand into the next two generations. Beyond his business accomplishments, Steve takes time to mentor younger men in leadership and discipleship. He plays a leading role in his church. He reads voraciously. He prioritizes a few deep, decades-long friendships. And perhaps most important, he models a thriving, long-lasting marriage for his children and grandchildren. At seventy-two years old, he shows no signs of slowing down.

Over the years, Steve has grown as a business leader without making irrevocable sacrifices in the most important areas of his life. That's not to say there haven't been challenges or serious bumps along the way. But unlike many business owners his age with a similar list of professional accomplishments, Steve does not have to look back over the last forty years and count the casualties he's racked up along the way.

What makes individuals like Steve successful is their capacity to lead. They do not constrain leadership to a single area or competency. It overflows into every area of life. Contrary to the contemporary tendency to define leadership in terms of business success, spiritual maturity, social influence, athletic prowess, or exemplary character, I want to argue in this chapter that great leadership is not isolated to specific areas of life. Effective leadership is all-encompassing, and it has distinctive traits we can identify and use to assess our own leadership capacity. But before we get there, let's understand why leadership is so important.

> *No matter what you are doing, great accomplishment requires great leadership.*

No matter what you are doing, great accomplishment requires great leadership. If you are leading a family, you must embrace the realization that the family's success cannot be dependent on your efforts alone. If you coach a high school football team, you can't win a state championship by putting on pads and taking the field by yourself. Similarly, if you own a business and want it to grow beyond your own abilities to sell and do the work, you must rely on the efforts of others. It will be your capacity to lead them that will determine how far all of you will go together. Without leadership, you will be limited in the scale of what you can accomplish.

No matter what we do in life, our ability to do more than we could by ourselves hinges on our ability to lead others. Yet somehow, we have managed to perpetuate a false notion that someone can lead in one area of life and be totally inept at leading in other areas. How many times have we seen politicians caught up in a sex scandal argue that their personal life has nothing to do with their political responsibilities? It is as if integrity had no place in evaluating their capacity to represent constituents. How many times have we witnessed business owners breaking through new revenue goals while their marriage and home life crumble?

Leadership follows us wherever we go. We are either good leaders or we are not. Failures of leadership in one area of our life inevitably act as precursors to future failures in other areas. Leaders like Steve are able to realize business success without making irrevocable personal sacrifices precisely because they do not draw a distinction between personal leadership and professional leadership.

I want to address what I consider to be five traits of effective leadership.

1. Great leaders are servants first.

2. Great leaders accept responsibility.

3. Great leaders are accountable to those they lead.

4. Great leaders are consistent.

5. Great leaders are coachable.

Great Leaders Are Servants First

In his book *Leadership Is an Art,* Max De Pree says, "The first responsibility of a leader is to define reality. The last is to say thank you. In between, the leader is a servant."

In these three sentences, De Pree breaks down leadership into three nice, discrete components. When leaders define reality, they are engaging in strategic planning, policy setting, and emphasizing values. This is all defining reality.

The first responsibility of a leader is to define reality. The last is to say thank you. In between, the leader is a servant.

It is a leader's responsibility to say thank you that enables leaders to amass a following. Leaders who are not humble and grateful endure constant turnover on their team. They must pay higher than market wages just to get people to show up for work. They complain about not being able to find good people. They arrogantly believe that those around them should just be thankful for the opportunity, and they don't understand why their culture is toxic to both employees and customers. Leaders who do say thank you are at the opposite end of the spectrum. They enjoy higher loyalty, better recruiting, and an infectious attitude that yields five-star customer reviews.

But it's the middle part, De Pree's statement that the "leader is a servant," that tells us what good leaders do most of the time. It is being a servant that makes the difference between great leaders and those who merely possess authority. After they have done the hard work of defining reality by setting a worthy vision, these leaders are able to entrust the day-to-day working out of that vision to the team. At that point, they show up every day and ask the question "What does my team need from me to be successful in their work?" This is what service looks like.

The problem is that most leaders do not define a vision for the team, or they define one that is not worthy of the team's best effort. Without ownership of the vision, employees are just work units to be deployed by the leader in whatever manner seems best at the time. They are pawns on the chessboard of the leader's making, and they require constant, vigilant attention and monitoring. The pieces in and of themselves are capable of little more than holding their place on the board. This kind of leadership is exhausting. It leads to frustrated business owners who can never find "good people" and who believe motivations like money and status matter most to employees.

Servant leadership is a popular ideal, but it usually falls apart because owners have not done the hard work of defining reality first. They have no compelling vision, they cannot articulate a shared set of values, and no one knows the mission. These leaders may sincerely desire to serve their people, but without any clear path toward the future, their employees honestly don't know what they need from the leader to be successful.

First, define reality in terms of values, vision, and mission. We discuss how to go about doing this in Chapters One and Two. Then serve with an attitude of humility. And don't be shy about expressing gratitude for the time and effort that people expend on your behalf. This is the foundation of great leadership—in small business, in politics, in large enterprises, in social institutions, in community organizations, in education, in professional sports … it is universal.

Servant leadership is a popular ideal, but it usually falls apart because owners have not done the hard work of defining reality first. They have no compelling vision, they cannot articulate a shared set of values, and no one knows the mission.

Great Leaders Accept Responsibility

For all of our talk about what good leadership looks like, there is one surefire way to spot poor leadership. Poor leaders always get hung up on who is at fault. They view accountability as getting to the root of the problem by identifying the culprits and bringing down the hammer. Good leaders, by contrast, understand that they are responsible for everything that happens on their watch. In so doing, they free themselves and those who work for them from the stigma associated with fault. By accepting responsibility, they take a huge burden off their managers and employees. This pays off in a lot of ways, one of which is that the people who do the work every day are not constantly looking over their shoulders. They can actually focus on the task at hand.

> *There is one surefire way to spot poor leadership. Poor leaders always get hung up on who is at fault …. Good leaders understand that fault is a dead-end road that will not lead to a solution or any type of personal development.*

Good leaders understand that fault is a dead-end road that will not lead to a solution or any type of personal development. It won't help the leader, it won't help the employee get any better, and it won't fix the problem. Some self-deprecating leaders believe it is admirable to accept fault for everything, but eventually they drive themselves into the ground and turn into beaten people no one wants to follow. Other leaders find fault with everyone but themselves and wind up creating a defensive culture.

In both cases, the person who suffered as a result of the mistake— the customer, a fellow team member, an upset vendor—is left sitting on the sidelines wondering, "Who is going to fix my problem?" My experience is that they usually end up fixing it themselves, sometimes by going somewhere else, sometimes by just going around the blame game and ignoring it. Either way, the relationship is damaged, and no one wins.

How much better would it be if the leader, rather than assigning blame, accepted responsibility and freed up those who had made the mistake to review the situation and understand what exactly went wrong (without any fear of consequence). Having done that, they would then be in a place to fix the situation and make it right. In accepting responsibility, these leaders "take the heat" and create space for their people not only to learn from what happened, but to come up with creative solutions to fix the problem.

People describe leaders who are willing to accept responsibility as unflappable, composed, self-assured, secure, and dignified. By contrast, those who place blame are characterized as frantic, manic, insecure, unprofessional, and distracting. Rather than take the pressure off their people, they turn up the heat and make finding a solution nearly impossible.

Someone told me once that if a baby is left on your doorstep, it is not your fault but it is your responsibility. In his excellent book *Boundaries for Leaders,* Dr. Henry Cloud recounts a story with one of his coaching clients. The CEO was complaining about his terrible company culture. As Cloud challenged him to just build the culture he desired, the CEO stumbled to come up with a reason he couldn't do that. Eventually he said, "You know, when you think about it … I am ridiculously in charge."

Cloud's insight that whatever exists in your business is there either because you built it or you allowed it to be built is at the root of accepting responsibility. (In Cloud's example, this applies to culture, but it is equally applicable in every area of your business.) Failure to accept responsibility is simply an acknowledgment that you are not the leader your business needs.

As a practical tip, I counsel my business owner clients to stop interrogating people who have made mistakes with questions like "Why did you do that?" Even worse, "What were you thinking?" These are blame-shifting questions. It doesn't really matter why they did it or what they were thinking. In hindsight we know that whatever they were thinking or whatever their motivations were, those things were clearly

Failure to accept responsibility is simply an acknowledgment that you are not the leader your business needs.

wrong. Getting them to say they were wrong one more time, in painful detail, only grinds them into the dirt even more. It is much better to ask, "What happened? What did we expect to happen? Where did we go wrong? What can we do to fix it? And, how likely is it that this will happen again?"

The posture of these questions is one of service. Help your people understand. Don't force them to accept blame. This requires that you take responsibility for everything that happens on your watch. In doing so, you will create space for your people to thrive.

Great Leaders Are Accountable

The idea that the boss is accountable to the people who report to him seems unconventional. But we need to go back to the start: What is your vision for the business? The people who work for you don't work for the paycheck. They don't work for the benefits. They don't work for the fancy Herman Miller chair you bought them last year or the dual-screen monitors you put on their desk. They can get those things, and probably more, working for someone else. Silicon Valley is full of employees with inflated compensation packages, crazy perks, and more amenities than you or I will ever be able to deliver to our own employees. And despite all that, those employees routinely leave to chase a dream at some new start-up with a vision to change the world in a new way. They aren't doing it for the money.

The people who work for you are volunteers. What will keep them with you is the worthy vision that you have invited them to help achieve. Therefore, if your vision is the reason they have volunteered their talents, enthusiasm, and best efforts, you too must be accountable to that vision. Otherwise, they will revolt. They will leave. They will fail to put in their best effort. They will withdraw their motivation, energy, and enthusiasm. You must act in a manner consistent with your vision if you expect them to help you get there.

It is hard to overestimate the importance of vision in creating a thriving business. When you fail to consistently pursue your vision, you owe your team an apology. You have let them down.

Most business owners think charisma is more important to leadership than accountability. In their view, the dynamic, polished, enthusiastic business owner is the one people want to follow. But charisma in the absence of accountability is dangerous. Cult leaders and crooked televangelists have loads of charisma and zero accountability. When they espouse a vision, it is self-serving and not worthy of the team's best effort. For these leaders, the vision is just a prop while they rely on their charisma to hold people in the group.

Accountability to a vision may sound warm and fuzzy, but like everything else we have talked about, it has practical consequences. Steve is a fellow CPA and a friend of mine who works with business owners on strategic growth and leadership. I was coaching Steve through a consulting project with one of his clients where he had to go out and interview several of the client's employees. After these interviews, Steve discovered there was one universal sore spot in the company. The owner of the business was an avid boater, and it seemed like he bought a bigger and bigger boat each year. The problem was that he parked his boat at the business, so every truck driver and technician drove by that boat twice a day. Do you think those employees were reminding themselves of the company's shared vision? Do you think they viewed their leader as accountable to something bigger than himself? Do you think they respected him? Steve learned firsthand from the employees that the owner's toys were one of the biggest culture killers in the business.

I am not saying that business owners who work hard, take risks, and make sacrifices should not enjoy nice things. What I am saying is that business owners who don't make accountability to a vision a personal standard cannot expect others to view their toys with the same sense of appreciation and gratitude. Even worse, business owners whose vision IS the acquisition of bigger toys create a toxic culture. The best leaders articulate a vision worthy of their TEAM's best efforts and make themselves accountable to both the vision and the team.

Great Leaders Are Consistent

I once knew a guy, we will call him Tom, who exhibited every appearance of professionalism and success. He was in charge of a multimillion-dollar organization. He was well respected among his peers in the industry. He surrounded himself with notable and accomplished people in the community. But a friend of mine is a school principal where Tom's kids go to school, and he told me about a different side to Tom. Earlier that week, Tom had been to the principal's office ranting and raving about the inadequacies of our school system, the incompetence of his daughter's teacher, the questionable credentials of the guidance staff, and the school's lackluster performance on standardized testing.

Tom went on to demand that his children be given preferential treatment. He backed up his demand with threats and claimed he knew school board members who could fire the principal with just one phone call from him.

A few months later I was sitting in the office of an attorney whom I'd never met before, and during casual conversation he discovered that I knew Tom. He told a story about Tom's antics at the recreational soccer field where Tom was known to belittle referees, second-guess coaching decisions, and make enemies of other parents.

When I heard these stories, it was hard to square them with Tom's business success. Revenues were growing, they were hiring people left and right, and their influence in the community seemed to be expanding. I wondered how Tom could lead this business to success in spite of the obvious flaws I was hearing about.

Had Tom simply been in the right place at the right time? He didn't start the business—he had been recruited and brought in as a successor. I wondered if he might be riding the coattails of his predecessor. I just could not imagine how anyone like the guy in these stories could be a good business leader.

Fast-forward a few years. Tom's business went stagnant. Turnover among leadership and front-line employees grew to historically high levels. Morale became nonexistent. Eventually, I was invited to take a look at the financial statements and give my opinion on the company's prospects. I saw decreasing revenue, declining cash balances, declining customer retention, and worsening overall financial health. Not long after that, Tom and his wife were divorced, his adult kids distanced themselves from him, and those closest to him started saying he was not the man they thought they once knew.

Great leaders are different. They take stock of every area of their life. They look for places where their leadership is lacking and needs improvement. They do not draw arbitrary boundaries between work and home, leisure and vocation. Like the proverbial canary in the coal mine, these leaders view small personal failings as pointers to areas needing improvement. I have seen several examples of this when working with business owners.

A lack of empathy at work may not cause big problems right away, but outside the office it will affect relationships much faster. Miles was often heard to utter the phrase "It's just business." He embodied the idea that it is okay to separate emotion from the workplace. But at home that same lack of empathy was killing his marriage and his relationship with his two teenage boys. To this day, Miles struggles to retain young talent among a generation that really cares if their work makes a difference.

Another example centers on greed vs. gratitude. An unwillingness to give in one's personal life, whether that be at the offering plate on Sunday morning or at the next-door neighbor's fundraiser, may highlight a greed or acquisitiveness that is also showing up at work. Everyone knew that Justin was a ruthless negotiator personally responsible for sealing some of the biggest contracts in his company. But they also avoided him whenever there was a collection for a sick employee or a community service project. In the office, a poor leader will try to justify this behavior as good stewardship, or sound capitalism. But it is unhealthy, and your team will notice when it shows up through unnecessarily harsh negotiations over pay or stinginess that keeps you from investing in the long-term health of the business, its employees, or the community.

Perhaps the biggest area I see leadership inconsistency play out with business clients is in the marriage relationship. Far from being disconnected from the business, this most critical relationship gives me a glimpse into what makes my client tick, and the areas they need to work on. A marriage is unique in that it provides both the opportunity to lead and the opportunity to be led. Great marriages are characterized by submission to one another. This submission is rooted in a shared vision of what the healthy marriage should be, not unlike the worthy vision of what a business should be.

A husband or wife who cannot be led by their spouse will not be able to put their own ego aside to serve others first. Nor will they be able to hire people better and brighter than themselves as the business grows. Dan and Sherry are a husband and wife client team who exemplify submission to one another. I've seen them lay aside ego and put the business and its team members first on many occasions. If you want to be a better boss, commit to be a better spouse first. If you can get that right, everything at work will seem like a cakewalk.

The main point is you should be the same person everywhere. A good leader is always trying to become better even when no one is watching and especially outside the office.

A good leader is always trying to become better even when no one is watching and especially outside the office.

Great Leaders Are Coachable

Being coachable requires the humility to admit that someone else knows more than you do even if they are not your equal on the playing field. We see this every day in professional sports. The coaches cannot perform the feats of athleticism and stamina that seem routine to the athletes on the field. Yet those athletes will defer to their coaches as having greater insight and understanding of the game. They defer to the coach even though they could destroy him in a game of one-on-one.

Do you believe that your wife, your pastor, your best friend, your mentor, your kids, or even perfect strangers can observe things about you that you can't see yourself? Do you think those things are relevant to your ability to grow as a leader and business owner? Coachable leaders appreciate those with the insight and courage to reveal their blind spots.

This kind of humility is not easy to exercise. It requires a drive and ambition to get better. When that drive supersedes your desire to be perceived as someone who has it all together, you will become coachable. You will ask people to critique your performance and give you honest feedback. Are you able to step out of your comfort zone and seek out or listen to critical advice? Or is it simply not worth the discomfort? Great leaders endure the discomfort, because their motivation to get better overrides their ego.

> *Are you able to step out of your comfort zone and seek out or listen to critical advice?*

But being coachable isn't just about taking counsel from others. At some point, great leaders must also coach themselves—by looking introspectively at their life and critiquing their own performance, and then having the grit and determination to go off and work on things by themselves. The best athletes know that the practice field is not the only place they have to put in the work. The coach may offer periodic critiques, but he's not in your face all the time. The best players stay after practice, after the coach has gone home and there's no one left to see them put in the work.

Do you spend time alone in quiet introspection and self-review? Do you hold yourself accountable to consistent standards in both your business and personal life? Do you read and study on your own to get better? Do you journal and take stock of what is happening in your life and how you respond to it? Are you able to distance yourself from the emotion of poor performance while you critique your work and put in the extra effort to get better?

Good leaders do all these things. They are coachable. When someone shows up in their life willing to coach, they take full advantage of the opportunity to get better. We started this chapter by looking at a friend of mine, Steve Wilson. Steve and others like him are not perfect, and they don't pretend to be. But Steve is a servant. He is willing to accept responsibility. He is accountable to his team. He is consistent across different areas of his life. And he is coachable.

> *Are you able to distance yourself from the emotion of poor performance while you critique your work and put in the extra effort to get better?*

Can you be successful in business while going through your fourth divorce? Can you be considered a good leader if you are estranged from your kids? Can you be a villain on your kid's soccer field and a hero in the boardroom? If we use a yardstick of financial profits and wealth, the answer might be yes, at least in the short term. But eventually it all shows through. For many of us, poor leaders are the reason we started our own business. We wanted to do it better, without the compromise, without the walls between business and personal, and without the wake of broken and damaged relationships behind us. I think leaders like Steve have it right. Leadership is not a nine-to-five job. Great leaders aspire to serve in a way that leaves the people and the things in their life better off than when they found them. Your people deserve a great leader. You were called to be one, and your company will thrive if you answer the call.

CHAPTER FOUR

Customers Come Second

Bernard was a demanding client, and he loved titles and accreditations. Each time we met, his business card always seemed to have a few more letters after his last name. While I didn't look forward to our meetings the way I did with some other clients, it wasn't an unpleasant experience. And the pay was good. Bernard always paid on time, and he appreciated the work.

But one day I heard some of our team members talking about Bernard. Specifically, they were recounting how he had spoken to someone on our team. Bernard had been demeaning, disrespectful, patronizing, and rude. I was surprised but not exactly shocked. I had met people before who would treat the business owner one way while treating everyone else like dirt. You see this a lot in restaurants where the server is treated like a second-class citizen, but when the restaurant owner stops by the table, everything changes.

I asked the team if I should fire Bernard as a client. They said no, he was too big of a client. I told them, "Forget about how big he is. Should we let people treat you this way?"

That afternoon, I called Bernard and told him we could no longer do his work. I did it diplomatically, but unequivocally. He was surprised, but it was my team that was truly shocked. That simple act of putting our team first and the customer second on that day did a lot to enhance our culture.

THE FOUR MAIN PILLARS TO LEADING A GREAT TEAM

Leading your team comes down to focusing on four main principles:

- Fulfillment
- Honesty
- Transparency
- Maintaining a loose grip

Fulfillment

Fulfillment is making sure that every team member is spending the majority of their time in their highest and best use. Highest and best use is a key standard that should apply to everyone in the company. It means identifying what each employee does best and evaluating whether their current role allows them to spend a significant amount of time in that sweet spot.

If the answer is yes, fulfillment demands that we raise the bar even higher so that employees are challenged to continually improve. Just spending time in your sweet spot is not enough. Either your competency within that sweet spot needs to deepen or your sweet spot circle needs to widen.

Just spending time in your sweet spot is not enough. Either your competency within that sweet spot needs to deepen or your sweet spot circle needs to widen.

Highest and best use addresses fulfillment because it is primarily concerned with the interests of the employee rather than the employer. We want the talents and abilities of our team members to be put to use. It means a lot to the long-term success of the business, but it also means a great deal to the short-term, day-to-day fulfillment experienced by the employee.

Taking a highest and best use approach does have its pitfalls. Often you will find that people are not in their highest and best use. What then?

If the business is big enough, it may be possible to find a different seat on the bus. There might be another position that is better suited to the employee.

But smaller businesses must face the reality that without an endless supply of seats on the bus, team members who are not engaged in their highest and best use may need to get off the bus. The struggle here is helping business owners understand that you aren't doing the employee any favors by letting them stay on your bus if there isn't a seat

You aren't doing the employee any favors by letting them stay on your bus if there isn't a seat where they can experience fulfillment.

where they can experience fulfillment. You may think it's cruel to ask someone to step off the bus, but it's far more sinister to allow that person to waste years of their life doing something they aren't good at, will never master, and that does not add richness and fulfillment to their work experience.

Step one is evaluating your individual team member's performance. To do this, business owners and managers MUST NOT think about how they will survive without a particular team member. Instead, they must assume that an A-player could step into that seat in the next thirty days. Here's why.

Business owners often fall prey to believing that any person in the seat is better than an empty seat. If that is your standard, you are passively choosing not to grow your business. Instead, you need to understand that while there might be some short-term inconvenience, you WILL be able to fill that seat with an A-player. So, evaluate performance against an A-player standard and be honest about whether someone is in their highest and best use.

If someone isn't meeting an A-player standard, step two is deciding whether there is another seat on the bus for them. Here you must evaluate the needs of the business first. Too often, I see business owners try to create a seat out of thin air so that they can avoid step three. Don't do that. By creating a position your company doesn't need, you are only delaying the inevitable and you are doing more harm than good to your employee's career. If there is another seat, move the person into it and hold them accountable to an A-player standard.

Step three is taking responsibility for the process of moving someone off the bus if there isn't an available seat. As discussed earlier, responsibility is different from fault. It might not be your fault that someone isn't at their highest and best use, but it is your responsibility. Get busy, tap your network, and help them find a place to land where they can start experiencing fulfillment and intrinsic value in their work.

It should be said that all of this is predicated on the assumption that you are dealing with team members who share your values. You should be willing to move heaven and earth to help these people land on their feet if there isn't a place for them in your business. But those team members who are not a culture fit should be moved off the bus long before you start asking any questions about highest and best use.

Honesty

A lot of business owners pride themselves on being able to give people honest feedback—which, to them, describes their ability to tell their team members things they don't want to hear. By calling it "feedback," they also give themselves permission to be completely oblivious to what the other person is feeling during the process. Naturally, a lot of employees hear the words "honest feedback" and cringe, because honest feedback is criticism wearing a professional mask. Employees don't want your honest feedback—they want your help.

When I talk about honesty, I am talking primarily about creating an environment where you allow your employees to be honest with you about what they need to be successful.

When I talk about honesty, I am talking primarily about creating an environment where you allow your employees to be honest with you about what they need to be successful. With our clients, I try to make things as simple to execute as possible, and this particular idea could not be simpler.

How often do you ask your employees, "What do you need from me to be successful?"

How often do you ask your employees, "What do you need from me to be successful?"

The frequency with which that question is asked and answered will determine the extent to which you create an environment where employees feel comfortable communicating their needs with frank honesty. It also determines how involved your employees are in your company's growth.

- If you ask it once a year, your employees will be involved in the bigger picture planning and goal setting that happens on a once-a-year basis.

- If you ask it once a quarter, they will be involved in the setting of priorities that contribute to the annual goals.

- If you ask it once a month, they will help you hit monthly metrics and targets that keep you on pace with priorities and goals.

- If you ask it once a week, they will be successful executing the plans and driving the actions that result in growth rates seen in the top 10 percent of companies.

- If you ask it daily, they will be successful setting their individual priorities and will stay focused on their highest and best use. More importantly, you will be able to give them the things they need to not only succeed, but to experience fulfillment.

Asking this question daily is a tall order. It is a commitment that most business owners will not make toward the growth of their business. But asking weekly is table stakes for building a team whose members can be honest with each other. Every week, you should be asking your direct reports, "What do you need from me this week?"

Some leaders push back on this as one sided, asking, "Well, what are they going to do for me? What about their responsibilities to the business?" Asking what your employees need opens the door for accountability. If the business owner is willing to be held accountable to deliver on the employee's request for help, the employee is also signing up to be held accountable to deliver on their end of the bargain.

The key to understanding accountability is to recognize that it is voluntary. If I want you to hold me accountable, I must voluntarily choose to be honest with you about whether or not I've done my part, what is getting in my way, and where I have failed, misunderstood, underestimated, overshot, wrongly assumed, and procrastinated. Because if I choose not to be held accountable, it is easy to lie, mislead, fudge the numbers, create plausible excuses, distract, misinform, and skirt the real issues.

By leading with the sincere question "What do you need from me?" the business owner is extending the invitation for honest communication that enables the employee to respond by volunteering to be held accountable. If the business owner doesn't deliver for the employee or if the employee doesn't deliver for the business owner, each understands that they can expect to be called out. That is accountability. And it doesn't have to be a confrontational or stressful exercise. Someone didn't follow through on their promise. Just talk about it and how to fix it. Honest communication is the basis for accountability. It's also the basis for great relationships. Why shouldn't business owners and employees have both?

Transparency

Transparency doesn't mean opening up every detail of your financial or personal life to every team member. All good leaders should be models of discretion, recognizing what information is appropriate to share with whom. But while discretion is admirable, secrecy undermines leadership. If there are areas of your business you don't want anyone to know about, that is a red flag for your leadership. Below is a short list to consider.

Are your employees paid market rates?

One of the first things we ask for when working with a new client is an organization chart that includes compensation information for every position. And what we find is that there are almost always individuals in the company who are wildly under-compensated. Eventually it will come to light that you are taking advantage of these team members. Not only will the revelation damage your leadership and credibility, it will probably leave you with a vacancy to fill. If you are embarrassed to have others find out what individuals are being paid, you lack the transparency that enables top performance. And you should stop kidding yourself. Your employees know a lot more than you think they do. We often find that everyone is aware of these payroll secrets anyway.

Are you stepping out of your comfort zone and sharing financial information with your team?

One of my favorite books is Jack Stack's *The Great Game of Business*. Open-book management is one of the best ways to engage your team, but it does take time. Start by sharing sales numbers and asking your team to take part in goal setting around revenue. Then move on to gross profit and bring them into discussions about how to improve on industry averages. Finally, address areas of overhead that they can influence. Most owners are scared to share financial information, because they think it feeds the perception that the owner is getting rich. That perception already exists, even if the company is break-even. You are better off trusting your team and asking for their help with the numbers.

Do your employees know your vision?

We started this book by discussing the role and importance of vision, yet it is incredibly common for business owners to keep their vision to themselves. Some do it because they are embarrassed to share their biggest hopes and dreams. They fear criticism or the potential to be judged as failures if they don't make it. Some have a vision that is all about themselves, and they rightly understand that sharing it won't increase morale. Some don't want to be held accountable to a vision. They would rather have the freedom to put the vision aside on days when they're not quite feeling it. But being transparent and sharing your vision is the

Being transparent and sharing your vision is the only way you are going to enlist the best efforts of those who will help you get there.

only way you are going to enlist the best efforts of those who will help you get there.

Are your employees constantly surprised
(and not in a good way)?

Transparency means sharing information as soon as it is feasible to do so. I've seen business owners "forget" to mention the opening of a new location. It is not uncommon for people to find out the company was interviewing for a new general manager only after they see a name plate going up on an office door. Salespeople don't know that the company set a new sales record last month. Employees read about lawsuits against the company in the newspaper. Coworkers find out someone was let go only after asking why they haven't been at work for several days. These are all examples of a lack of transparency that leaves your people reeling and wondering if you really care about them. Don't take for granted the effect that sharing news has on your team. They want to know, and you need to make the effort to tell them.

Maintaining a Loose Grip on Your Employees

There is a realization that you must come to as a business owner. Most really good team members are going to grow personally and professionally faster than your company's ability to provide highest and best use opportunities for them. This means that the majority of the bright rising stars in your company will be with you for a time and then will need to move on. If you care about them, you will embrace this truth.

Leaders who maintain a loose grip take the time to find out what drives their employees' motivations, what they aspire to, how they grew up and what their family expects of them, where they want to live ten years from now, how their career is affecting or will affect their spouse and children, what books they read, where they go to church, why they go to church, what they view as their biggest weaknesses, and what keeps them up at night. This sounds like a tall order, but it's not. It is literally one or two intentional conversations laid on a foundation of fulfillment, honesty, and transparency.

The best leaders build this foundation not to make the most profits, but to EXPAND their mission. What better way to expand your influence than to train and equip the best A-players, enjoy the fruits of their labor for a time, and then send them off to do great things elsewhere? It truly is a small world, and these leaders know that in some way, shape, or form they will always be connected to the extraordinary results their A-players achieve, whether or not those A-players are still on the payroll.

The Dead Sea is a good analogy for this loose grip approach. The Dead Sea is a giant lake in the Middle East that has no outlet. The Jordan River flows in, but nothing flows out. The result is a chemical composition in the water that insures nothing can live there. No fish, no birds, nothing. You cannot drink the water. You cannot use it for irrigation. It's called "dead" for a reason. Businesses must encourage their best performers to move on when the opportunities run out. Otherwise they risk becoming dead zones, avoided by the A-players and left to mediocre performance by people who don't aspire to personal or professional growth.

The day I fired my client Bernard was the day I realized that my customers had to come second. I started to share a lot more financial information with team members. We implemented daily huddles where I asked, "What do you need from me today?" I started having intentional conversations with team members about what they aspired to and how Axiom fit into the bigger picture of their lives and aspirations. And I started to encourage some of them to pursue bigger and more promising opportunities. To this day, I tell my teammates, "I want you to stay here forever, but that's probably not going to happen. I'll give you 100 percent and you do the same. Eventually, if we need to go our separate ways I'll move heaven and earth to help you in any way I can." I've never been disappointed in their response.

Part Two

HOUSEKEEPING FOR A PURPOSE

CHAPTER FIVE

Create the Playbook

If you watch a group of kids playing football on the playground, you'll see one kid drawing in the dirt telling everyone else where to go. The plays are uncomplicated, and they change from one kid to the next, from one day to the next. This kind of impromptu play-calling may work great in elementary school, but NFL players are expected to memorize a playbook that can be inches thick.

Professional football teams aren't the only teams that need a playbook. Every business needs one, covering things like hiring practices, customer service, how products get delivered to the customer, the different ways customers pay us, where things are kept in the warehouse, how to schedule time off, and so on. The playbook is one of the things that separates the amateur from the professional. It is what makes the difference between a well-run business and one that is constantly inconsistent.

Besides being inconsistent, businesses that don't have a playbook rely on a few people to know everything. These superstars—we call them Aggregators—manage to keep operations afloat, but when they leave, all hell breaks loose. Relying on Aggregators is managing by personality rather than managing by process. The attitude of Aggregators is often that "it's easier to fix stuff than it is to train others to do it differently." One of our clients had an incredibly talented bookkeeper who was also a notorious Aggregator. Every Friday, the office became a zoo as this Aggregator processed payroll. She allowed supervisors and foremen to submit their departmental payroll on sticky notes, Chick-fil-A napkins, the back of old work orders, or anything else they could find laying around. It was a disaster, but the bookkeeper corralled it all and just made it work.

> *The attitude of Aggregators is often that "it's easier to fix stuff than it is to train others to do it differently."*

We stepped back and asked, "How should this be done?" With our help, the bookkeeper designed a form for the crew leaders to complete, and she assigned each crew leader a five-minute window on Friday mornings where they could submit payroll for their department. Everything was typed up and rolled out during a special meeting with all the supervisors and foremen. Within a few weeks, payroll went from an all-day affair to a routine one-hour weekly task that could be done by any of three or four people in the office.

The playbook is the conduit through which you can communicate a great deal of your experience and knowledge. Your team still needs individual attention, training, and mentorship. But if they get it alongside a good playbook, they will develop much faster and your business will see the results much sooner. Building your playbook doesn't have to be hard.

The following is a formula that works well for small businesses:

- Decide what comes first.

- Decide where to build it.

- Checklists: your secret weapon.

- How-tos: making it all work together.

- Pink notepads: refining as you go.

What Should Go in the Playbook First?

The first thing that needs to go in the playbook is the thing you do "one hundred times per day." If you are a pest control company, it is how to do a pest control stop. If you are a roofing company, it is how to put on a roof. If you are a dentist office, it is how to clean teeth.

Every business must do a lot of things and do them well, but there is always one thing that the business does most often. You should start with that and move on from there. In a roofing company, we might start with putting on a tile roof. Later we can address shingle roofing, sales proposals, diagnosing leaks, ordering materials, handling customer complaints, payroll, and so on. The earliest things you tackle with your playbook should be the things that are most relevant to DAILY business operations.

Next come the things you do routinely but less often. You put these processes in the playbook because they save time, eliminate mistakes, and increase quality. A good example is hiring new employees. By documenting the recruiting and hiring process, a business can eliminate a lot of the haste and inconsistency that results in bad hires.

Several other areas you should consider for your playbook include your monthly process for closing the books, the monthly cleaning checklist for the warehouse, the quarterly maintenance schedule for fleet vehicles, your monthly check-in with your highest-value customers, and semiannual facilities inspections and cleanings.

Eventually your playbook will cover things you do less frequently. These are things you can forget how to do because you don't do them very often and include things like preparing to file your tax returns, renewing insurance contracts, setting annual bonus amounts, getting ready for the company Christmas party, renewing licenses and permits, and renegotiating merchant accounts with your credit card processor. Documenting these tasks saves you enormous time, because you don't have to keep reinventing the wheel after forgetting how you did it last time.

Every business has hundreds of processes it must contend with. Our goal is not to put everything on hold while we push paper and create checklists. Our goal is to bring consistency and effectiveness to as many parts of the business as we can, starting with those parts that will have the biggest overall impact.

Every business has hundreds of processes it must contend with. Our goal is not to put everything on hold while we push paper and create checklists. Our goal is to bring consistency and effectiveness to as many parts of the business as we can, starting with those parts that will have the biggest overall impact. Start with the thing that is most important, and once you have been able to celebrate some progress, move on to improve another area of the business by adding it to the playbook. As the playbook grows and becomes more comprehensive, you and your team will experience a growing sense of competency and confidence when it comes to your core operating procedures.

Deciding Where to Build the Playbook

Now that you have an idea of what goes in the playbook, let's talk about the nuts and bolts of how to put one together. The most important thing about your playbook is that everyone knows where it is located. Early on, you need to decide whether the playbook will be physical or virtual. The decision is yours to make, but I will outline a few things you should think about.

Physical playbooks are usually easier to start but more difficult to maintain. If you have a very small office where everyone has access to a work room or file room, a physical playbook can be the way to go. Something as simple as a three-ring binder that contains all of the latest processes and checklists will be all you need. Low-tech options like this are pretty easy to understand, access, and update.

The downsides of using a physical playbook include the fact that only one person can use it at a time, and if you have employees in the field, they won't be able to get to the playbook. Of course, you could create a playbook for each employee, but this leads to a second disadvantage of physical playbooks. They are difficult to scale across larger workforces. If you have twenty people in your company, it may seem easy enough to give everyone their own physical playbook. But early on, you are going to have a lot of updates to your playbook. Rolling these updates out across twenty different field copies can become a nightmare. A crucial change to one of your most important forms or processes may never make its way into every playbook. The goal is to have everyone performing a given task in the same way, and that is not always possible if you have to distribute updates and make sure they get added to multiple copies of the playbook floating around in field trucks.

There is one more reason I hesitate to recommend a physical playbook to most businesses. Physical playbooks lend themselves best to plain text. That doesn't mean they can't incorporate rich media, but color pictures and diagrams are about as far as you can take a physical playbook. Eventually, most businesses will want to incorporate things like training videos and online resources into their playbook. Physical playbooks just can't do this.

The other option is a virtual playbook that users can access through desktops, laptops, tablets, or phones. Software programs and online services exist specifically for this purpose, but my preference is for more generic solutions. For the most part, our clients use a shared folder structure on their server or a cloud storage service like Dropbox for Business, Box.net, or Google Drive. Everyone on the team can be given access to a hierarchy of folders that contain the most recent updates. Content can consist of text documents, spreadsheets, presentations, videos, websites, online forms, pdf documents, audio files, and so on.

A well-organized folder structure eliminates the need for a separate table of contents. However, we do recommend that you create a document that will serve as your master index of processes. The master index should include the name of the process, the version number, the date that version was created, and the person or department that is primarily responsible for maintaining the process. It's very helpful to be able to scan down this list of processes and differentiate those that are relatively new from those that have not been updated in years. Older documents may not need to be updated, but it is helpful to be able to review the list at least once a year and ask "Is there anything here that is terribly out of date?"

Every playbook needs a good custodian who makes sure that the index is kept up to date. This is usually an office manager, but whoever serves as the custodian must be organized and willing to champion the playbook as a way to improve the business. The custodian will work with department heads to make sure that versions are documented and that any new updates are included in the playbook.

Sometimes business owners hesitate to develop a comprehensive playbook out of fear that some rogue employee might steal all their secrets and hand it to the competition.

Sometimes business owners hesitate to develop a comprehensive playbook out of fear that some rogue employee might steal all their secrets and hand it to the competition. That might be a possibility, but it would mean that you did an exceptionally poor job of hiring and judging the character of your team members, and that is something that is entirely under your control. Regardless of whether the occasional bad apple sneaks through your hiring process, the fact is that operating without a playbook does more harm to your business every day than you would ever experience from one or two leaks to your competition. And remember, the playbook only says what to do; it's up to you and your team to do it in a way that creates happy and loyal customers.

Checklists: Your Secret Weapon

When it comes to documenting processes and building your playbook, there are few things more effective than a checklist. If your playbook consisted only of the essential checklists needed to run your business, it would be an invaluable tool for everyone on your team. Checklists are easy to understand and provide a step-by-step process with instructions for team members to double-check their work. This helps them perform tasks consistently and accurately.

When it comes to creating checklists, I like to divide them into four parts.

THE TITLE

The title should be descriptive but succinct, using as few words as necessary. I also like to include the word "checklist" in the title. A good checklist title might be "Checklist for Making Customer Service Appointments." Anyone who happens across this part of the playbook will know exactly what it relates to and how it is supposed to be used.

THE SYNOPSIS

The synopsis is important because it communicates how you want the checklist to be used. The synopsis should be no more than two or three sentences. For our previous example of customer service appointments, the synopsis for the checklist might read as follows:

"This checklist is meant to help you communicate with the customer and assure them that we understand their needs and will respond on a specific date and time to meet that need. It is important that you remain upbeat during the call and maintain an air of confidence and competency at all times."

THE OVERVIEW

In the overview, we are looking for just five to ten major bullet points. Again, going back to our previous example, the overview might look something like this:

- Answer the phone with confidence.

- Gather the customer's information.

- Locate the record in the database.

- Enter the service appointment information.

- Confirm with the customer.

- Send information to the service technician.

- Confirm that the information went to the service technician.

- Enter notes that will help the salesman on the next call.

THE LIST

The final part is the checklist itself. It should list, in detail, the steps required to complete the task. Let's go back to our example one more time and look at a checklist similar to one created by a client. We aren't going to create the whole checklist, but let's look at just the first step in the overview: answer the phone with confidence. Our first two checklist items might address this step as:

- ✓ Always answer the phone with your headset in place so that you do not have to put the customer on hold and so that the customer has a consistent call quality experience.

- ✓ Answer the call using the appropriate greeting as outlined in the "call scripts" section of the playbook.

We want to provide enough detail to remove ambiguity but not so much that we are trying to turn our employees into robots. The

The more detailed your checklist, the more easily it becomes outdated.

more detailed your checklist, the more easily it becomes outdated. Try to strike a balance between providing useful detail and not getting stuck too deep in the weeds.

How-Tos: Making it All Work Together

Checklists are useful because they are brief and because they describe things in bullet points that can be read quickly. Some items in a checklist may only consist of one or two words (for example, "Confirm address"). But there are times when you need more information. So much work today is done on computers, tablets, or mobile phones. For documenting this type of work, pictures, screenshots, slide presentations, and screencasts do a much better job than words alone. We differentiate these items from checklists by calling them "how-tos." So when we have a how-to for "Booking a Service Call," it will include detailed pictures of the relevant computer windows along with descriptions for each field, rules for what constitutes valid information in each field, what different buttons on the screen do, and so on. How-to documents are longer and more tedious than checklists. Their purpose is for initial training and future reference, whereas checklists will be used every day. How-to processes will only be referenced when someone has a question or isn't quite sure how to handle an edge case.

Usually the best way to assemble a how-to is to just to go through the process and record the steps as you go. How-to documents take a lot longer to create than checklists and require a good bit of patience. The first draft will inevitably contain gaps and mistakes.

Video is another powerful how-to medium, whether the process happens behind a computer screen or out in the real world. In the time it takes to do a service call, a helper with an iPhone can record the technician demonstrating exactly how to do the call in the exact level of detail that will be required in the field. If you use video, don't worry about fancy graphics or visual effects. Keep the videos short—two to five minutes is best. Make sure you have good audio, and don't worry about much else. Get two takes. The second take is always more succinct and on point.

Screencasts are the video equivalent when processes involve work on the computer. Software programs like Screenflow record everything happening on the screen and provide the ability for video and audio accompaniment.

Pink Notepads: Refining as You Go

Every business owner and manager I work with is interested in ways to limit and even eliminate interruptions. Over the years, we have come up with a powerful method for tweaking the playbook and cutting down on interruptions at the same time.

Your most experienced employees and managers are bombarded by questions that will only take "two minutes." It is easy for their day to become consumed by two-minute questions, and the most frustrating part is that most of these questions are repeats of two-minute questions they've already answered. We give these managers pink legal pads to leave on top of their desks.

Each time someone comes in with a "two-minute" question, the manager asks them to wait while they write down the question on the pink notepad. The manager then answers the question and as briefly as possible writes down the answer on the notepad as well.

Once a week, the manager meets with the team and brings along a typed list of the "frequently asked questions" (FAQs) from the notepad. During the meeting, each question and answer is covered briefly. After the meeting, the custodian adds these FAQs to the relevant sections of the playbook. Over time, the FAQ sections of the playbook become some of the most valuable, for new hires and long-term employees alike.

Why does this work so well? First, it puts the employee asking the question on notice that their question is being written down and will be the topic of group discussion later in the week. This has the effect of making employees think twice before they barge into the manager's office with a silly question they know they could find the answer to with a little effort.

Second, it allows you to build the playbook very efficiently. You could spend a lot of time trying to anticipate the most important questions your team needs answered. Or you could just let them ask, write down the answers, and put them in the playbook.

Over time, your playbook will create a competitive advantage for your company. It will allow you to train new employees to be productive more quickly, resulting in lower hiring and training costs. It will create more consistent experiences for your customers, resulting in higher retention and more referrals. It will reduce errors and rework and all the costs that go along with them, improving your bottom line. The important thing is to start today and start small with the thing you do a hundred times per day. Come up with the checklist first. Then develop a how-to that shows employees the standard you expect. Back it all up with FAQs from actual experience. Very quickly, you will see marked improvement that goes directly to your bottom line.

CHAPTER SIX

Customers Are Real People

Sooner or later, businesses that desire growth must shift their focus from inside processes to outside sales. Growth requires a steady stream of customers making consistent purchases. As simple as it may sound, getting clear about exactly what you are selling and exactly whom you are selling it to is the first step toward growing sales.

Small business owners know their customers. This is mostly because the business owner is the salesperson-in-chief, who may have been the single point of contact for most customers for years. They know their customers' families, their likes and dislikes, their product purchase histories, and their budget constraints. But often when they step into the conference room to design a sales and marketing program, they lose that personal perspective.

Customers are real people. They think like real people and make decisions like real people. They like to hear their names. They like predictability and certainty. They enjoy personal connection. And your sales and marketing process should acknowledge all of that humanity and personality. The more you focus on exactly who your customers are and what you are selling them, the more effective you will be.

The secret sauce behind most small business growth is the ability to scale up a marketing and sales function that can consistently provide new customers. That program must preserve the personal relationship. It's not enough to have the personal touch without process, and it's not enough to have process without the personal touch.

Two friends of mine, both financial planners, exemplify this difference. Dave has become very clear about who his customers are, what he sells them, and how he does it. Jason has a broader definition of who his customers are, provides a much broader range of services, and is known for exceptional service and personal attention. Both have done very well. But Dave's business is growing at an extraordinary rate.

Dave's clients are former blue- and gray-collar retirees. They are retired school teachers, firefighters, policemen, construction foremen, executive assistants, and government workers. All of them are or soon will be receiving Social Security. Almost all of them moved to Florida from the Northeast. Almost all of them have grandkids out of state. They were taught to live on less than what they earn and to save the difference. And they have done that for the last thirty to fifty years.

Dave finds these clients by offering free monthly seminars on retirement and social security. He is a masterful communicator. He is on a mission to make sure these people who have sacrificed so much finally enjoy their retirement. Dave's message is "Enjoy your retirement and stop worrying about running out of money."

Interested attendees are invited to schedule a consult with Dave. If things move forward from there, they become a client over the next thirty days. This sales and marketing program has worked so well that Dave needs to hire new people to take care of his ever-growing list of new clients.

Jason's approach to growth is much different. He is looking for new financial advisors who will go out and find their own clients. While Dave has figured out the process for getting new clients and needs lower-skilled people to take care of them, Jason hasn't figured out how to get new clients and needs expensive professionals to get their own clients—hopefully these expensive professionals will stick around Jason's firm long enough for him to enjoy some of the shared profits.

Dave has a marketing and sales process. Jason does not.

> There are four fundamental pieces to a good sales and marketing process in your business:
>
> 1. Your offer
> 2. Your value
> 3. Your pitch
> 4. Your delivery

Your offer is the thing you are trying to sell. Dave and Jason are both selling financial planning and asset management services. But Dave has gotten much more specific—he has narrowed his offer to cover only a subset of the things Jason offers. He knows his customers don't need all those things.

Your value is the reason clients should trade their money for your product or service. They will only do that if they believe that what you have to offer is more valuable to them than the money they have to spend. Dave's value is the security and peace of mind to retire without worry. That peace of mind is worth more to his clients than the 1 percent per year that he charges them.

Your pitch is the method you use to ask clients to spend money with you. Dave's pitch is his series of seminars and follow-up meetings. Each one is well rehearsed, consistent, and repeatable.

Your delivery happens after the customer signs on. It is made up of the product they take home, the service they enjoy, and all of the subsequent interactions you have with them. Dave's delivery is built on reinforcing the peace of mind and security he built up as the main value in working with him.

Developing a marketing and sales process for your business does not have to be extraordinarily complex or expensive. You don't need experts or college degrees in marketing. You DO need to sit down and think deliberately about these four areas, and I'm going to walk you through each one.

Your Offer

When it comes to what you are offering your customers, are you offering them too little or too much? Almost always, the answer is that you are offering them too much. The most successful small businesses get very specific about what they offer and whom they offer it to.

A great example of this is the contrast between the two restaurant chains Five Guys and Steak and Shake. Both have hamburgers at the center of their menu offering. Yet Steak and Shake has managed to add just 550 locations over the last eighty years, while Five Guys has added over 1,500 in less than half that time.

Steak and Shake sells everything from hamburgers to pancakes. Five Guys sells burgers and the occasional hot dog.

Steak and Shake has counter seating, booth seating, table seating, and drive-through service. Five Guys has no drive-throughs, no counter, and seat yourself/clean yourself/bus yourself tables.

Steak and Shake positions their restaurants predominately at busy interstate highways and caters to everyone from truckers to teenagers and soccer moms. Five Guys restaurants are almost always in strip centers situated in middle- and upper-middle-class shopping districts.

To start building clarity around your offer, you need to think first about your CORE offering. Every business has core offerings and additional offerings. Five Guys's core offering is burgers, but they also sell milkshakes. Dave Kennon's core offering is financial planning, but he also sells life insurance. If it is hard for you to pick one product or service as your core offering, that is the first indication you are spread too thin, you don't have a core offering, and your business is going to be hard pressed to grow.

If it is hard for you to pick one product or service as your core offering, that is the first indication you are spread too thin.

Small business owners are notorious for underestimating the importance of having a single core offering. One of the hardest things we do is try to convince business owners that it is necessary to prune services and products to grow the company. Author and consultant Mike Michalowicz turned this idea of pruning into a book. The entire premise of *The Pumpkin Plan* is that the only way to grow a 300 lb., blue ribbon-winning pumpkin is by killing off (pruning) all but the single healthiest pumpkin on the vine.

Sound ruthless? It can be. But think about all the time, energy, and money being sucked up by non-core offerings. If you stopped doing those things today, you would take a revenue hit. But you would also realize immediate cost savings and focus your effort on areas of the business that actually produce profit. Our experience with clients has overwhelmingly shown that pruning reduces short-term revenue, increases short-term profit, and drastically increases long-term revenue AND profit.

When we talk about pruning, we are talking about moving from being a generalist to a specialist. And at the economic heart of the argument for specialization is the reality that focusing your efforts results in lower costs and higher revenue. Here's what happens when you specialize:

1. Specialists can perform the service or deliver the product faster with less turnaround time. Because of this, they are able to command a premium price.

2. Specialists focus their spending and are able to obtain necessary products and services at lower costs.

3. Specialists have a narrower target market, enabling them to focus their marketing and sales promotion dollars, ultimately spending less and achieving more.

4. Specialists are "top of mind" with their customers and referral partners and generate more word-of-mouth business than generalists.

5. Specialists have shorter sales cycles, enabling them to convert prospects to customers much faster due to the fact that most prospects have already "prequalified" themselves as good customers by showing up at a specialist.

Right after starting my own firm, I got to work with one of these specialists, and they are still a client today. David and his partners are roofing contractors, but they specialize in elastomeric metal roof coatings. These products extend the life of a metal roof by fifteen to twenty years.

During my first visit to their nondescript office, I was impressed by the aerial photos of job sites hanging on the walls. I saw picture after picture of gleaming white roofs on warehouses, manufacturing facilities, condo buildings, self-storage properties, aircraft hangers ... they were everywhere. David explained how he paid a couple hundred dollars to get high-quality aerial photos before and after every job.

David created a postcard mailer and contracts with a direct mail company. With just a couple of days notice, he can have the direct mailer send out ten thousand postcards to metal building owners in any area of the Southeast that has experienced heavy rainfall during the past week. Not long after these mailings, the phone will start ringing. Because David speaks the language and knows exactly what a leaking metal roof can do to a distributor's inventory or to a manufacturer's equipment, the sales process is fairly quick.

Today, David's portfolio of aerial photographs covers hundreds, if not thousands, of properties. He doesn't have to send out as many mailers today; if you own a twenty-year-old metal building in the Southeast you probably already have his name on file. If your metal roof leaks, there's a good chance you know where to find David and his company, Unicoat Industrial Roofing Corp.

What makes David special? He knows what his core offering is and he sticks to it. He knows who his customers are, and he knows what they need most from him. Knowing your core offering and whom to offer it to is the first step in creating an efficient sales and marketing engine.

Your Value

The second piece of your marketing and sales process is your value. There is only one reason customers will do business with you: they value your product or service more than they value the cash in their pocket. We experience this every day as customers ourselves—for example, the gas in my tank is more important to me than the $50 it takes to fill up the tank. David's customers place a high value on dry inventory and equipment because without those things their business literally grinds to a halt.

Fundamental to your value proposition is your pricing. It is possible to charge so much for a roof coating that customers would rather have soggy inventory. But the inverse is also true. When you underprice, your customers wonder if you know what you are doing. They worry that your product is of poor quality. They become skeptical and generate more customer service inquiries and warranty claims, even when the product isn't at fault.

Pricing is mostly art and a little bit of science. The science is knowing your costs. If you set your price below your costs, you won't be in business very long, so know your costs. After your costs are covered, the question becomes "What is the market price?"

To find the answer, you have to ask the market. You can do this by consistently raising prices and measuring when sales levels finally start to drop off, or you can go talk to real customers and get real, honest answers. My experience is that most businesses will not do the hard work to find out the answer to this question. Whether they are too busy or too uncomfortable, they just won't do the work to find out. Those willing to do the work usually crush their competition.

Do the work. Call twenty customers and have real conversations with them about what they value in your service, how much you save them, how much revenue you generate for them, and what nonmonetary benefits they get from working with you or from buying your products. What don't they want to pay for? What are they frustrated with? How much more would they be willing to pay or recommend that a friend pay if you fixed all the frustrations they currently have?

If you ask these questions, there is a good chance you will find out that you are underpricing. This happens so often because to the roofer, a roof isn't that big of a deal. But to the person with water pouring through the ceiling, it's a huge deal. To the CPA, a tax return isn't a big deal. But to the client, the stress of an IRS audit and all those incomprehensible forms is a huge deal. Your customer doesn't take your product or service for granted like you do. My plumber wouldn't even consider paying someone $100 to fix a leaking pipe, but to me it's a bargain.

Do the hard work. Go out into the market and find out what the value proposition is for your core offering and set your prices accordingly.

Do the hard work. Go out into the market and find out what the value proposition is for your core offering and set your prices accordingly.

Your Pitch

The third piece of your marketing and sales plan is your pitch. I use pitch to cover everything from your advertising all the way through to closing the sale. Just like determining your value, most businesses will not do the simple but hard work required to perfect their pitch.

There is a simple way to tell when your pitch is ready, even if your product or service isn't available to ship yet. When ten people have said, "Take my credit card number and charge me when you deliver," you know your pitch is ready. You might need to have one hundred conversations to get ten credit card numbers, but those one hundred conversations are gold! In them, you will hear the language your customer uses to describe their frustrations. You will understand the problems your product solves and the language the customer uses to describe those solutions. You will discover the features that no one really cares about or is willing to pay

When ten people have said, "Take my credit card number and charge me when you deliver," you know your pitch is ready.

for. And you will take all that information as it comes in and you will refine your product and your pitch as you go.

Your pitch should also be consistent and repeatable. Consistency is important because as you measure results, you want to be able to make small changes and measure their effect. Over time, you can hone your pitch and train others to deliver it just as consistently as you do. That is how you build a sales force. You also want to be able to iterate on marketing plans and advertising. To do that, you need consistent execution and consistent measuring of results, so you need to know your numbers. You should be measuring everything that has to do with your pitch, including the following:

1. The number of leads coming into the business on a daily, weekly, and monthly basis.

2. The average cost of each lead.

3. Your top five lead sources and the number of leads produced by each.

4. The number of proposals or pitches given.

5. The close rate on those proposals.

6. The amount of your average sale.

7. Your average sale frequency per customer (how many times the average customer buys from you in a year).

Do the work no one else is willing to do, and you will get the results no one else seems to be able to get. Every one of these numbers is available to the business owner willing to go get it.

Do the work no one else is willing to do, and you will get the results no one else seems to be able to get.

Your Delivery

The final step is delivery, because if you can't deliver on your sales promises, your marketing and sales process (and your business) will be short-lived. We have already talked about this regarding the playbook, but it belongs here as well. You must have a process for delivery that can keep up with sales. That isn't to say that things will always run smoothly. It is entirely normal for a growing business to experience the growing pains of backlogs and longer-than-expected lead times. But if your product or service is fundamentally flawed, the best marketing and sales program will be useless.

Do you deliver the product or service consistently? Do you have a section of your playbook dedicated to it? Do you follow up with customers to make sure your value proposition is still relevant? Do you track your numbers closely enough to quickly spot small problems before they become huge ones? Do you have a pitch that is documented so that you can tweak it and work toward continuous improvement?

If I go back to Five Guys, it isn't because I admire the concise menu or the focused core offering. It is because I know I'm going to get a good hamburger. And if I ever fail to get a good hamburger, it's going to make me think twice about going back. I probably will, but maybe just once. If they let me down twice, there are plenty of other options.

It is common for a business to struggle with the two competing priorities of chasing the work and doing the work. To escape this cycle, you must have the discipline to work on the marketing and sales process. Once you make the transition, you will have a consistent stream of new customers coming into the business and an operations team capable of getting all that new work out the door. Undertake the building of your marketing and sales process deliberately by addressing each of the four areas: offer, value, pitch, and delivery.

The Secret Ingredient

I want to say one more thing about bringing the marketing and sales process together. It is the secret ingredient that sets one business apart from another. It is this:

A BUSINESS WITH A PERSONALITY WILL CRUSH A COMPETITOR WITHOUT A SOUL.

Personality comes down to ten simple habits. We notice them every time we see them. We talk about them to our friends and neighbors, and we mention them in online reviews. We come back to businesses over and over because these things cover over a multitude of sins—everything from expensive prices to botched delivery can be overcome by these silver bullets of personality:

1. Let customers hear the sound of their own name.

2. Say hello and goodbye and mean it.

3. Look customers in the eye when you talk to them.

4. Smile.

5. Say something, anything, other than a canned response.

6. Say thank you.

7. Apologize and ask forgiveness.

8. Talk good about your customers behind their backs.

9. Ask if there's anything else you can do to help them.

10. Give them a gift every now and then to show your gratitude.

If any of your employees are incapable or unwilling to do these things, they have no business interacting with customers.

If you don't see people on your team doing these things, it is because you aren't showing them how it's done.

If you think this stuff is too hard or not worth your time, there's a competitor out there that's glad you are lazy.

Not long after college, I realized that there were two types of CPAs. There were the stereotypical spreadsheet types that loved bank reconciliations and tracking down every last penny. They were the heart of the firm and the ones that clients wanted working on their books. They were never happier than when they had a full inbox and a quiet day ahead of them. We'll call them the bean counters.

Then there were the CPAs who had full calendars. They spent their days meeting with clients, taking prospects to lunch, and managing the teams of accountants and CPAs doing all those bank reconciliations. We'll call this group the rainmakers.

I noticed that bean counters all worked in cubicles and the rain-makers all had offices with windows. I also noticed that while the clients *said* they liked the bean counters, they never called and asked to speak with them. They always called and asked to talk with the rainmakers.

My point here is twofold. First, CPA firms realized early on that there were some people who were better at dealing with customers than others—the rainmakers. But they also realized that they needed the bean counters to build a successful firm. And they put those people in the right seats.

The second point is that the market placed a much higher value on the rainmakers. Their ability to deal with customers placed them in higher demand and enabled them to command higher salaries.

In your marketing and sales program, you cannot ignore the fact that some of your people shouldn't be doing much with customers and others should be working almost exclusively with them. As the leader, it's your job to put people in the right seats and give them the tools they need to succeed. In this respect, effective marketing and sales is as much about putting people in the right spots as it is about having the right process.

CHAPTER SEVEN

Get Out of the Way

Todd runs a company that manages manufactured home communities. This includes keeping the books for each community and preparing a detailed set of financial statements for the board of directors each month. Todd's goal was to deliver financial statements to the communities by the twenty-first of each month. But it was rare for that to happen, and Todd's team wanted to improve their turnaround time.

In our interviews with the accountants responsible for doing all of the work, we learned that they were called upon to perform a variety of non-accounting tasks during the day—things like covering the front desk, answering phones, and dealing with high-maintenance customers. As a result, they rarely had a quiet moment. This was not a situation conducive to focused, efficient accounting work.

We implemented several changes with Todd's team, but when we came back a month later to check on progress, there was one change that everyone was talking about. We had given the accountants red signs to hang on their door that read:

CLOSED DOOR TIME

I AM WORKING ON SOMETHING IMPORTANT AND WILL BE AVAILABLE LATER TODAY. THANK YOU FOR UNDERSTANDING.

They had been using these signs to limit interruptions and were already realizing significant improvements in the turnaround time on their monthly financial statement packages. In fact, they were delivering packages by target date each month and the team was making significant progress toward the new goal of delivering all packages within seven days of month end.

What we did with Todd's team was introduce a common language of time and task management. That language created an environment where clear and concise communication about needs and expectations became part of the culture. If your team is going to expand beyond your own abilities, this common language is essential. It doesn't matter whether the team is two people or two hundred. Their time and task management habits will drive or cripple the growth of your company.

Planning or Execution: Pick One

The first step in understanding why we need a good system for time and task management is understanding how your brain works. It can only do one thing at a time. It can work on planning, or it can work on execution. You have to pick one or the other.

As kids, we used to dare one another to flip the switch on the ceiling fan, not the on/off switch, the other one right next to the blades that controls which direction the fan is spinning. If you got it right, the fan would slowly stop, reverse direction, and start picking up speed going the opposite way. If you got it wrong you might lose a finger.

Your brain works the same way as that ceiling fan. When the switch is in one position, your brain is in planning mode. When it is in the other position, it is in execution mode. You can only do one at a time. You can plan or you can execute.

In planning mode, things start off slow as you sort through all the options and consider what things you could do. As you pick up speed, it becomes easier to think prospectively and to consider things like "If we want 'x' result, we need y and z to happen first." At full speed, you are able to see all kinds of options and opportunities.

But then you flip the switch over to execution mode and the fan slows down. It eventually stops and starts going the other way. Things start off just as slowly. You struggle to get traction and gain any momentum. It seems like it's taking too long to get stuff done. But after a while you are ticking things off the list and seeing the results of your hard work. You feel productive and accomplished.

When we think about how we spend our time, we need to deliberately choose planning mode or execution mode. And we need to stay in a mode long enough for the fan to get up to full speed. People without a plan are stuck, constantly flipping the switch back and forth. They finish one task in execution mode, then go back into planning mode to decide what to do next. Then they switch back to execution mode to get things done, then back to planning mode to decide what to do next. They never get up to speed, and both their planning and their execution suffer.

In this chapter, we are going to deal primarily with planning and execution on a daily/weekly basis, but the same lessons hold true for monthly, quarterly, and annual planning and execution cycles.

In this chapter, we are going to deal primarily with planning and execution on a daily/weekly basis, but the same lessons hold true for monthly, quarterly, and annual planning and execution cycles.

Effective Planning and Execution

When it comes to planning and execution, there are several best practices that can help you get the fan up to full speed. This is not meant to be a comprehensive resource, but rather a practical one. With just a handful of basic principles, you can enjoy the freedom to experiment with different systems until you find the one that works for you. These best practices will provide the common language of time and task management your team needs to be most effective.

Planning best practices:

- Keep a to-do list.

- Block your time.

- Make a short list.

Execution best practices:

- Keep the plan in front of you.

- Stay put.

- Expect interruption.

- Close the door.

Communication best practices:

- Ask with intent.

- Be explicit.

- Bring your list.

- Keep a calendar.

EFFECTIVE PLANNING

Keep a To-Do List

A to-do list is a necessity, because you need to put all those planning thoughts somewhere so that they won't be forgotten. The king of to-do lists and productivity for the last twenty years is David Allen, whose Getting Things Done system has developed a cult-like following. Allen's basic premise is that you need to get all of that stuff out of your head so that you can free up mental capacity to get things done instead of wasting all that energy trying to remember what you have to do.

Allen's book is an excellent resource, but it isn't the only approach. I don't care what method you use for keeping your list, as long as you follow two simple rules.

1. Everything must be written down.

2. It must be written down in the same place every time.

Writing commitments down is important, because if it's only in your head you can forget it. Your fellow team members need to have confidence that if your memory fails, something important isn't going to

Writing commitments down is important, because if it's only in your head you can forget it.

slip through the cracks. Hear this: If you are not willing to write down the things that you have committed to, you are letting your team down. If you think you can remember everything, you are being prideful. If you can't be bothered to write stuff down, you are being lazy. Your team will have more faith in you as a leader if they know you take commitments seriously enough to write them down.

Keeping everything in the same place is just as important. If your list is on a note card today, in your planner tomorrow, and on your smartphone a week from now, something important is going to fall between the cracks. You can switch systems over time, but those changes need to be deliberate. If you write things down on paper, keep everything on that paper. If you use an app on your phone, put everything in that app. If your company uses a team-wide platform, resist the urge to have separate lists somewhere else. Put everything in one place so that you know where to go to review your commitments.

If you write things down on paper, keep everything on that paper. If you use an app on your phone, put everything in that app.

Block Your Time

Time blocking is all about getting the fan up to full speed. When you do your planning, set aside enough time to really think through your important priorities for the day, week, month, quarter, and year. Then, organize your calendar to get 90–120-minute blocks of time when you can go head down without interruption and work on important projects.

One of the best ways to make sure you have the opportunity to time block is to set appointments with yourself ahead of time.

If I have a particularly important project deadline, I will make sure that I have several two- to three-hour blocks of time set aside on the calendar in the days or weeks leading up to the deadline. Everyone knows not to schedule appointments during these times.

With time blocking, you must take a proactive approach. If you have any level of responsibility in your organization, your calendar will be filled by others. Set aside the time you need to get your most important work done while leaving some time blocks open and available for others. Don't let everyone else fill up your days and weeks with less important (albeit urgent) matters.

Make a Short List

The short list is where planning mode meets your to-do list. While your to-do list may contain dozens to hundreds of items, there is no way for you to address all of them at once. Without a system for prioritizing what you can and should get done today, you will become paralyzed and default to putting out urgent fires.

> *One of the best habits any leader can develop is creating a short list of the most important tasks for the day.*

One of the best habits any leader can develop is creating a short list of the most important tasks for the day. You can also do this for the week, but daily is usually a first step. By limiting yourself to just three to six items, you will have more focus and purpose during the day, and you will be more aware of your tendency to address urgent matters on your list rather than the non-urgent but more important projects.

When we get business owners to start with a short list every day, two things happen. First, they realize just how much of their day is spent on things that they did not choose to spend time on. Managers and employees have a never-ending list of problems, issues, decisions, and opportunities that require your input, and customers have a never-ending list of requests, fires, complaints, re-orders, special orders, and "two-second" conversations they want to have. That's all before you have taken a single call from a salesperson or vendor. When you start with a short list, these demands on your time become more obvious, and you realize just how much you are at everyone else's mercy when you start without a clear sense of direction every day.

The second thing these business owners realize is that they will never get to the most important things on their list without some serious effort. It takes an ability to push minor and urgent decisions down the chain of command to free up significant time for non-urgent and important long-term focus. Urgent things still have to get done, but good leaders come to realize that doing urgent tasks is rarely their highest and best use.

The short list is where most business owners and teams either fall off the rails or realize huge improvements in productivity and effectiveness. If you can keep the list to your top three priorities, you are putting yourself in a position to say no to other important, but urgent, tasks. Be realistic about what you can get done. Each month has about twenty working days. At three important tasks a day, that's at least sixty high-value tasks that you can accomplish in a month. Few business owners think they have time to get sixty major tasks completed in a month, but they walk around every day with a to-do list that has dozens of "have to" items they never accomplish. Less is more. Limit yourself to three "must do" items every day. Your progress over the course of a month will be staggering.

Less is more. Limit yourself to three "must do" items every day.

EFFECTIVE EXECUTION

Now let's flip the ceiling fan switch. Just as there are best practices for planning, there are similar things you should be doing every day on the execution side. Let us assume you are keeping a to-do list, that you have blocked out enough time to get up some momentum, and that you have three items on your "must do" list for today. How do you get it done so you can go home feeling like you have done your best work?

Keep the Plan in Front of You

I am a technology and gadget nut. But when it comes to my plan, I like tangible things I can reach out and touch, pick up, put in my pocket, and lay down in plain sight. Once you enter execution mode, your plan needs to be front and center where you can't ignore it. It might be an index card with your short list. It might be a planner page that has your schedule and short list written out next to each other. It might be a sticky note. Whatever it is, don't enter execution mode without the plan in front of you where you can see it.

> *Once you enter execution mode, your plan needs to be front and center where you can't ignore it.*

It is important to have the plan in front of you, because you will get interrupted. You will get distracted. You will have things come up that tempt you to spend the afternoon putting out a fire or entertaining a drop-in guest. One glance at the plan and you will see these for what they are: tempting distractions. What seems like an urgent fire to put out will become something you can delegate to someone on your team. It is often said that to say no you need to have a more compelling yes. The plan is your compelling yes, and it will empower you to say no more often.

Stay Put

Once the switch has flipped, let it stay on execution. Resist the urge to do a midday review of your entire to-do list. Don't get sucked into pulling up your calendar and doing a bunch of time blocking for the next two weeks. Don't start grouping and reorganizing project folders. Remember, once in execution mode, your brain is spinning in a certain direction. It is in the here and now, not the prospective world of planning. Stay with it, and don't go back to planning mode until you can tick off all the items on your short list. Even then, you should probably stay head down knocking other items off your longer "would like to do" list.

> *The hardest time to stay in execution is at the beginning of a task and especially at the very beginning of your first task of the day.*

The hardest time to stay in execution is at the beginning of a task and especially at the very beginning of your first task of the day. Recognize that you are getting the fan up to speed. Push through and stay with the task no matter how hard it seems. At these times, it's much easier to slip back into planning mode under the pretense of working smarter, not harder. However, there is a place for this. I call it micro planning, and it can overcome some of the friction of starting on a new project. If you have set aside a couple of hours to work on a bigger project, take two to three minutes to think through the steps and develop a mini plan of attack. Then once you start, don't turn back. Eventually the fan will get up and running, and the momentum will carry you through to completion.

Expect Interruptions

You will get derailed. Part of being great at execution is being able to put your work aside for a moment, then pick up where you left off with a minimal loss of momentum. When you have the plan in front of you, it becomes much easier to address the unexpected interruption. That plan becomes the anchor that keeps you from drifting too far off course. It allows you to set things aside and be fully present with those who legitimately need to interrupt you. The plan sitting there in front of you creates an urgency to handle the interruption as quickly as possible. And once done, it tells you where to jump back in to stay on course.

One of the consistent pieces of pushback I get from business owners is that there's no way they can anticipate everything that's going to happen during the day and plan for it. And that is exactly my point. There's a part of the day we can plan, and there's a part of the day we can't. Understand that, and use the plan as a tool to get back on track after interruptions. Don't get frustrated.

Close the Door

I make no apologies for the fact that I think an open-door policy is a terrible idea. It is often trumpeted as an integral part of a company's culture. I hear managers and owners brag, "And we have an open-door policy around here," like it is on par with the 401(k) plan and a major reason people come to work there. We might as well celebrate water cooler gossip and twenty-minute smoke breaks. They all have the same effect on productivity and effectiveness.

In any serious company, everyone needs closed door time. It doesn't matter if you are in leadership or production. Uninterrupted time to focus on important tasks and projects is essential if your team is to work effectively. Every time I see the bookkeeper in a company covering the phones I cringe. Do you really want the person doing payroll to get interrupted ten times an hour?

Business owners fight me on this consistently. But the ones who take me up on it quickly become believers. Here are some ground rules to make closed door time work for your company.

CLOSED DOOR TIME SHOULD BE EXPLICIT. Make a big red sign and hang it on your door. Seriously, this is no time for subtlety. Build a common language to explicitly communicate closed door time and use it.

CLOSED DOOR TIME SHOULD BE COORDINATED. Someone needs to be available to handle phones, emergencies, interruptions, and so on. Let your people work together to set up closed door time for each other so that they can cover one another and serve each other.

CLOSED DOOR TIME SHOULD BE LIMITED. It only works if people know you are going to come up for air at some point and become available again. The person who leaves the closed door sign up all the time can expect constant interruptions as people become immune and ignore it.

CLOSED DOOR TIME HAS TO BE RESPECTED. If everyone pays attention to the sign except the boss, it's no good. It only takes one person breaking the rules to sacrifice all the benefits of closed door time.

EFFECTIVE COMMUNICATION

One of the reasons we address time and task management at the team level is that without a common language it is impossible to communicate needs and expectations clearly. Everyone can have their own individual systems, but at some point they have to come together and function as a team. Here are some basic principles that foster clear communication at the team level.

Ask with intent

Before asking someone to get or do something for you, consider whether you can get it yourself. If you can't get it yourself, is it so important that you need to interrupt what the person is doing right now? Often we go to others because we are either lazy or impatient, or we have procrastinated too long. Waiting until the last minute is a major reason we need someone to do something for us NOW. Don't be lazy. Get it yourself, wait for it, or plan ahead next time.

Be explicit

Remove ASAP from the company vocabulary. It is too subjective. Your ASAP and mine are almost certainly different. This is especially true with email. Make a habit of indicating your needed time frame in the subject of the email. It is very easy to communicate "need this a.m., need this p.m., need in one day, need in one week." Don't make team members guess. Remember, your pressing need is usually the result of procrastination and a lack of planning.

> *Make a habit of indicating your needed time frame in the subject of the email.*

Bring your list

Team members who show up to meetings without their to-do list should be sent back to get it. If commitments are going to be made, those responsible for them need to write them down. It is pointless to have a meeting, make decisions about what needs to get done, and then risk that something is going to fall though the cracks. If people can't be troubled to bring their list, they don't take their commitments seriously. If they don't take their commitments seriously, they don't deserve a seat at the table.

Keep a calendar

Meetings and appointments go on the calendar. Period. And the first rule of keeping a calendar is to have only one. Keeping one calendar on your phone and one on paper is a recipe for disaster. But regardless of the method or technology, everyone is responsible for keeping their company calendar and hard commitments. No excuses. People who don't keep a calendar miss meetings and waste everyone's time.

How to be taken seriously

Jerry was a sales manager at one of our clients. Every time we would meet with the team, the other four managers in the room made a habit of bringing their to-do lists, including follow-up items from our last meeting, but not Jerry. Jerry would show up empty handed and offer insights into whatever issues were being discussed, but when we went around the room to follow up on prior commitments, he could rarely report any progress.

John was the controller for the company and a meticulous note taker. One day, I noticed that John would write down both the things he was committing to and the commitments of his fellow managers. But he stopped writing whenever Jerry would make a commitment. He had so little faith that Jerry would follow through that it wasn't even worth his time to write it down. I began to notice that no one really took Jerry's commitments seriously, and they didn't acknowledge any of the points he made when we were discussing strategy or basic business issues. About a year later, Jerry was fired. There wasn't any one issue or event that lead to his dismissal. There was just a sense that he wasn't up to the caliber of his fellow managers.

Failure to master time and task management is ultimately a failure to live up to your commitments. Over time, it eats away at your effectiveness and your credibility. In a manager, that can be a major setback to growth. In a leader, it is a fatal flaw. Decide today that you and your team will make time and task management a core competency in your company.

CHAPTER EIGHT

The Coach Always Knows the Score

Jessica had found herself in the right place at the right time, and business was good. She was smack in the middle of an aging baby boomer population, in the heart of one of the country's most desirable retirement communities. It wasn't a surprise that her home health care business was experiencing double-digit growth for the fifth year in a row. The problem was just keeping up with all the new business coming in.

As we got involved in the business, I started to work with Kathy, Jessica's right-hand person and general manager. In our meetings, I would ask Jessica for ballpark estimates on accounts receivable or overhead spending, and every time, she would turn to Kathy. Kathy knew all the numbers, but that was a problem.

Being able to get the number is not the same thing as knowing the

Being able to get the number is not the same thing as knowing the number.

number. If you know the number, it affects your behavior. If you have to go get the number, you usually don't bother. That means business owners who don't know their numbers consistently act or plan without the benefit of critical information.

As the company continued to grow, Kathy struggled to keep up. Jessica was forced to jump back in and take a more active role. What she found surprised her. The company was hurting in several areas, from revenue and receivables to out-of-control overhead spending. She admitted to me that if she had known the numbers, she would have stepped in earlier or coached Kathy to be more disciplined with the finances.

This chapter is about understanding a handful of critical numbers in your business. Like the coach of any team, you should always know the score. You can delegate a lot of things, but knowing the score is not one of them.

Many of these numbers come directly off the financial statements. Others are a combination of financial numbers and operational numbers. All of them are accessible and practical if you take a little time to understand why they are important. That is my goal—not to make you an accountant, but to give you enough knowledge that you can put your accountants to good use. Those who know the numbers can also see when someone is trying to use overly complicated financial explanations to skirt the real issue. Your BS detector is about to get a whole lot better.

> *Those who know the numbers can also see when someone is trying to use overly complicated financial explanations to skirt the real issue. Your BS detector is about to get a whole lot better.*

Daily Cash Balance

This one is easy. The saying "Cash is king" became a cliche for a reason. When cash runs out, operations grind to a halt. But other, more insidious things start to happen before cash runs out. When cash is low or unpredictable, it affects the ability of any business owner to think long term. We make poorer decisions. We fail to take advantage of opportunities. We get short with our teammates. We become anxious and distracted around our family. As a result, the position of many business owners is "ignorance is bliss."

My friend Jamie had an El Camino in high school, and it had a broken gas gauge. Jamie knew that no one else was going to fill the tank, so he kept his eye on the odometer, doing the mental math to know when we needed to find a gas station. Too many business owners are blindly relying on someone else to fill the tank.

At the start of every day, the business owner should know, to the penny, how much cash the business has in its accounts. With online banking and today's software programs, there is no reason cash cannot be reconciled daily. We have businesses that routinely process two hundred cash transactions on a slow day, and their daily cash reconciliation takes less than fifteen minutes.

Several things happen when a business owner starts receiving a daily cash balance. First, there are fewer surprises. One of our clients was surprised when his bookkeeper came in and told him the company had missed three months of sales tax payments. She was about to send $320,000 to the state, including several thousand dollars in penalties. If our client had been in the habit of getting his daily cash balance, he would have noticed that for three months his bank balance did not decline as much as it usually did around sales tax payment time. Instead, he got a nasty and expensive surprise.

Second, when receiving a daily cash balance, you begin to build an expectation of what a "normal" balance is. When cash drops below this normal balance, you start asking questions about receivables, about large expenditures, about contracts in the sales pipeline. Knowing the daily balance can create a sense of urgency and purpose, especially when it drops below normal levels.

> *What you measure and pay attention to improves. And it all starts with knowing the daily cash balance.*

Third, "normal" tends to go up over time. Owners in the habit of reviewing a daily cash balance watch spending more closely, collect money more quickly, and watch their balances go up over time. What you measure and pay attention to improves. And it all starts with knowing the daily cash balance.

Daily Sales

Dan is a client I usually meet with once a month, and we always meet toward the end of the day, about the same time his last customer is checking out at the front desk. Right after the start of our first meeting, Dan paused, picked up the phone, and got the day's closing sales number from the front desk. I knew right away we were going to enjoy working together.

The daily sales number is the pulse of the business. It tells you whether all that busy activity actually resulted in anything productive. It lets your team know that you are paying attention. It keeps you and everyone else focused on the activities that will result in tomorrow's cash balance being better or worse than it is today. And it is usually one of the easiest numbers to get.

A common complaint among business owners is how long it takes them to get their financials from accounting. It is not uncommon for small businesses to wait three to six weeks after month end to get their numbers. But if they start receiving their daily cash balance every morning and their daily sales number every evening, things drastically improve.

They still need to get their financials out earlier, but 90 percent of what they need to know they can get every day. If they have a revenue target for the month, they know by the end of every day whether they are on track. And if they have cash flow issues, they know at the beginning of every day just how low the cash balance is.

When you get right down to it, nearly all of the costs of a business are known well ahead of time. Rent is the same every month, utilities are roughly the same every month, payroll is roughly the same every week or two, paper clips cost about the same, and gas and cell phone bills rarely yield surprises.

The biggest culprits for cash flow surprises are poor sales and major expenditures. By tracking daily sales, you will keep from falling behind revenue forecasts. By tracking daily cash, you will control major cash outflows. And whether your financials are ready at the end month or not, you won't need them to understand how your business is doing.

Gross Profit Margin

When we explain the income statement to clients, we divide it into two halves. The top half contains gross profit (revenue minus cost of goods sold). The bottom half shows overhead spending. We will talk about the bottom half in the next section.

The top half of the income statement describes how your business is performing against the industry standard. This is useful because, to a large extent, the market determines pricing. You may differentiate at the top or bottom end of the market, but there is a range of prices for businesses that do what you do.

The market also tends to determine direct costs. The direct laborers who work in your industry generally make about the same amount of money regardless of which company they work for. Some make more, some make less, but across the range there is an average. Similarly, there is a cap on what distributors can charge you for raw materials and supplies.

So, since the market sets the prices in your industry, and the industry uses roughly the same products and vendors, and the labor pool is about the same … you can expect that your gross profit is about the same (or should be) as other industry players when stated as a percentage of revenue.

Occasionally a business will enjoy a real competitive advantage. If you have a patent on your product, you might be able to charge significantly more because no one else can offer it. If you own a sister company that provides your raw materials, you may be able to purchase them significantly cheaper than the competition. But in the world of small business, this generally isn't the case. When we compare the gross margin (gross profit divided by revenue) of businesses within the same industry and geographic market, they tend to be very similar.

This means that a $1 million business and a $10 million business have roughly the same DIRECT cost structure. I know there are economies of scale that can reduce costs, but on the whole, the top half of your income statement looks a lot like your peers' *on a percentage basis.*

Knowing your gross margin is important because it lets you know whether you are out of touch with the industry or not. If your gross margin is low, there are only two ways to fix it: (1) raise prices or (2) lower direct costs. If your gross margin is high, you should be able to explain why and if it is sustainable. Otherwise, you may be in for a rude awakening as customers flee to cheaper competitors for essentially the same product/service.

> *Knowing your gross margin is important because it lets you know whether you are out of touch with the industry or not.*

You should know your gross margin at the end of every month and for the twelve months ended with the most recently completed month. If you do project work (as opposed to selling widgets), you should be measuring the gross margin of each completed job to avoid any nasty surprises and to spot trends as they happen. You should also know the gross margin for your industry, section of the country, and company size. Trade associations are a valuable resource in this regard. The NYU Stern School of Business maintains a list of industry gross margin statistics at http://pages.stern.nyu.edu/~adamodar/New_Home_Page/datafile/margin.html.

Overhead Spending Against Budget

The bottom half of the income statement covers overhead spending and net income. This is where individual differences and preferences of the owner stand out. One business may be perfectly fine with eight hundred square feet of sparsely furnished office space and vehicles that have two hundred thousand miles on them. However, the competitor down the street has plush office space and brand-new trucks.

Both businesses earn the same revenue, both have the same gross margins. But one will have a significantly higher bottom line because overhead spending is kept lower.

There is a lot to talk about in overhead, but the most important thing is this:

OVERHEAD SHOULD BE BUDGETED.

All this means is that we decide ahead of time what we will spend money on for the next year and then measure differences from this expectation. It is the same as a household budget. Let's say you budget $800 per month for meals and entertainment. It is now the fifteenth of the month and you've already spent $750. If you want to stay on budget, you and your spouse will probably think twice before going to a fancy restaurant.

Businesses that operate without a budget are most likely using their cash balance to make spending decisions. If the cash balance is high, they spend money. If the cash balance is low, they don't spend money. The problem with this approach is that it doesn't consider the seasonality of revenue or large annual expenses like income taxes. But that's not the biggest problem. **Businesses that fail to budget fail to spend money in places that will grow the business.**

Growth requires investment, and investment comes from profits. Businesses that budget control spending to achieve a minimum of 10 percent net pretax profit. This means that if a business is generating $1 million in revenue, it will control overhead spending to achieve a minimum pretax profit of $100,000. Why a minimum of 10 percent?

Uncle Sam is going to want about 3 percent of that 10 percent for income taxes. If the business has any debt, another 2 to 3 percent is required for principle payments. Hopefully the business owner is putting away 2 to 3 percent minimum for unexpected expenses and rainy day funds. That leaves 1 to 2 percent for the business owner to take out as dividends. As you can see, a business earning 10 percent net pretax profit is essentially treading water. If a business wants to grow, it really needs to be earning 15 percent net profit margin. That additional cash is invested back into the business through marketing, additional salespeople, new equipment, and so on.

Break-Even Sales

If a business has a revenue forecast (which should be easy to come up with once you get in the habit of reporting daily sales), if it knows its gross margin, and if it has budgeted its overhead, the business owner has the equivalent of a green and yellow light traffic signal. If daily sales are meeting forecast, gross margin is normal, and overhead spending is in check, the light is green. If any of those areas is off, the light is yellow. But what about the red light? Enter break-even sales.

Break-even sales are the level of sales at which the business does not earn a profit but also does not lose money. The powerful thing about break-even sales is that they can be calculated for virtually any time period, from yearly break-even sales all the way down to hourly break-even sales. Think about a drive-through fast food restaurant. If the business knows the portion of its daily revenue that is typically earned during the lunch rush (and believe me, it does), it can come up with the number of hamburgers that need to go out the window every hour from 11:00 a.m. to 2:00 p.m. to avoid going into bankruptcy. This allows managers to watch daily sales during the lunch rush and see trends far enough in advance to adjust schedules, change pricing, launch promotions, or add a second order window. Break-even sales are powerful tools.

Break-even sales are calculated by dividing overhead spending by the gross margin percentage.

For a business with 40 percent gross margins and $1,000 per day in overhead, the daily break-even sales are $2,500 ($1,000 / 40 percent = $2,500). You can work backwards to prove this out. Revenue of $2,500 times gross margin of 40 percent less $1,000 of overhead = $0 of net profit.

To calculate *annual* break-even sales, divide annual overhead by gross margin. To calculate *weekly* break-even sales, divide weekly overhead by gross margin. You can use break-even sales for any time period to determine whether the red light is flashing or not. Businesses that do not use break-even sales to manage operations will typically enjoy fat profits during the busy time of year and give much of those profits back when things slow down. Their competitors know when the yellow light turns red, and they immediately begin to adjust labor schedules, cut overhead costs, and adjust prices to bring in just enough business to keep from losing money. At the end of the year they have enjoyed the benefit of the fat, profitable months while avoiding the bloody, unprofitable season.

Understanding Your Balance Sheet

I stood looking out at a dozen business owners, all more accomplished than me. One headed a $150 million construction firm. Another had been in business for over forty years. Another had started and sold four businesses in the last twenty years. These people were giants to me, and I respected all of them. They had asked me to come and repeat a talk I had done on helping business owners understand financial statements.

As we went through the income statement, there were a lot of nodding heads, and I could tell they grasped the material well. I had no doubt that many of them were already doing some of the things I was suggesting. Then we switched gears and I said, "Let's talk about the balance sheet. By a show of hands, how many of you are completely comfortable with your balance sheet, meaning you understand what the numbers represent and how they got there?"

One hand went up. These guys ran multimillion-dollar companies, and almost none of them understood one of the most basic financial statements in the business.

I have learned that this is pretty common. The income statement makes sense. Revenue minus expenses equals profit. This looks a lot like the real-world experience of receiving money from customers and paying out some of it to vendors and employees. The rest, we get to keep. It is never *that* simple, but the income statement is arguably easier to understand than the balance sheet, so most business owners stay clear of the balance sheet.

It is important that you understand your balance sheet, because without it there is a hole in your financial understanding of the business big enough to drive a truck through. At the simplest level, the balance sheet is made up of just three things:

- Assets—what you own.

- Liabilities—what you owe.

- Equity—what you are worth.

The three are related mathematically in the equation A-L=E (or to the accountants as A=L+E).

If you have $100 in the bank, that is an asset, something you own. If you owe the credit card company $120, that is a liability. If these are your only balance sheet items, your equity is negative

$20, meaning that you're not just broke, you're on the verge of bankruptcy. Let's talk about each of these in a little more detail.

Assets consist of cash, accounts receivable, inventory, equipment, and deposits you have with utility companies, landlords, and so forth. These are all things you own.

Liabilities consist of accounts payable, credit card debt, bank loans, payroll liabilities, and prepayments from customers for which you have not yet delivered products and services.

Equity consists primarily of capital you invested in the business and retained earnings (profits from previous periods that you have left in the company and "retained").

If you think of your balance sheet this way, it makes it possible to sit down with your CPA and ask questions like "Accounts receivable is something I own, right? It's an asset? It says here that we have more than $300,000 in accounts receivable, but we only sell about $1 million a year to customers. Are you telling me we have the equivalent of four months of sales that is still out there uncollected?"

This conversation actually happened with a friend of mine, and what he found out was that for years his company had been failing to collect from certain customers, but that they continued to sell to those deadbeat customers. He made phone calls to the owners of these customer companies, asked why the bills hadn't been paid, explained he had little choice but to stop doing business with them if they couldn't get current, and added $150,000 to his bank balance over about two weeks.

Armed with this very simple understanding of your balance sheet, you should have the conversation line by line with your accountant or bookkeeper. And don't stop asking questions until you are satisfied with the answers.

Armed with this very simple understanding of your balance sheet, you should have the conversation line by line with your accountant or bookkeeper. And don't stop asking questions until you are satisfied with the answers. The next time you are in a room with eleven other business owners, you will be the one person who actually fully understands what is happening in the business.

THE PRICE OF NOT KNOWING

Asking owners to invest this time is a hard sell, until they have a war story to tell. Occasionally we run across corporate fraud. In one case, a bookkeeper embezzled $200,000 over the course of two years. In another case, a bookkeeper embezzled over $400,000 in about the same amount of time. These were small companies, and the losses nearly put them out of business. In both cases, a full understanding of the financial statements would have caught the fraud earlier or prevented it altogether.

It may not be as sinister as embezzlement. It may be that your bookkeeper gives intentionally confusing answers to get you to go away when you ask tough questions. One time I overheard a business owner ask the bookkeeper, "How come we are so busy but the cash balance isn't going up?" The response was "That's just because we are on a cash basis of accounting instead of accrual." And the owner just nodded his head and turned the page. I wanted to yell something across the room and tell the bookkeeper he was full of it. But this wasn't a client. I was just a customer waiting for them to finish washing my car, and I didn't want to cause a scene.

The point is that you should understand your numbers and stay on top of them. If you don't and there is someone else in your company who does, it is a recipe for disaster. If you don't understand your numbers, your business is adrift and it might not survive when the unexpected happens. Knowing your numbers not only gives you resilience, it puts you in a position to grow.

Part Three

GROWING WITH PURPOSE

C H A P T E R   9

What You DON'T Do Matters Most

I tell the business owners we work with the same thing all the time: "What we do isn't rocket science, but it is a discipline." And the key discipline that enables company growth more than anything else is focus. Focus is not the opposite of distraction, it is the antidote to distraction. Without focus, you are sure to catch the disease of distraction. It is guaranteed.

Strategy is just a fancy name for focus. When we decide to focus on a strategy, we are also saying that we will not be distracted by things that don't have anything to do with that strategy. The problem in almost every business is that, over time, so many things compete for the leader's attention that no single area ever sees great progress. Business success is more often a marathon than a sprint. Businesses we admire have been around for decades. Certainly there is time to narrow our focus for a few quarters on one or two specific areas so that we can make real progress.

Larry is a great example of focus. He moved to southwest Florida and eventually bought a real estate brokerage from one of my clients. When Larry arrived on Anna Maria Island and started sitting in on real estate closings, he noticed something. Most of the closings were for vacation rental properties and there were three parties at the table: the seller, the buyer, and the buyer's property manager. The real estate agents representing the buyer and the seller split about 6 percent of the sales price. But the property manager was a different story.

The property manager's job was to list the vacation rental, take bookings from guests, and manage the vacation house throughout the year for the owner. And for that, the property manager would receive 17 to 20 percent of the annual rent income, plus expenses ... every year! It didn't take long for Larry to figure out which seat he wanted at the table. So he started a vacation rentals business inside the real estate brokerage.

In the beginning, Larry focused on one thing—marketing. He drove as much traffic to his website as he possible could. He improved the number and quality of photographs that vacationers could view online. He outspent competitors on web advertising. He locked up high-quality domain names and redirected them to his site. He optimized content to drive organic search results. And the bookings came.

Then Larry had another problem. Every property had to be cleaned and readied for new guests on Saturday morning. He was forced to manage a slew of independent cleaning companies. He dealt with inconsistent quality and the headache of managing multiple vendors. So he turned his focus to cleaning. It took a couple of years, but when he was done, Larry had hired his best cleaning subcontractor and made her his new star manager. All of those vendors were turned into employees where Larry could control training and scheduling. Eventually his team could turn over properties on Saturday faster than any competitor on the island.

Then Larry had another problem. The cleaners had developed a system to increase efficiency. First, they would strip the linens and put them in the washing machine. Next, they would pull a fresh set of linens out of the closet and change all the beds. Last, they would clean the rest of the vacation house. But every time, they were stuck waiting for the old linens to dry so that they could fold them and put them away before locking up the newly cleaned rental. Larry talked to other vacation rental companies around the country to see how they had solved the same problem. Over the next few years, he installed industrial washing and drying equipment, built a new building with a first floor dedicated to linens, and drastically cut the turnaround time for his cleaners. They now carried fresh linens to each property, stripped the beds, changed the linens, cleaned the house, and came back with dirty linens that could be washed before the next week's Saturday cleaning. The system was so successful that Larry's competitors started paying him to do their laundry as well.

Larry recently sold the business to an international company. The buyer recognized the value he had built after ten years of methodically focusing on one thing at a time. During those ten years, he passed up real estate deals, enticing proposals from software vendors, management fads, potential acquisitions, distracting opportunities for side businesses, and geographic expansion. Instead, he dug deep. He focused on boring things like spreadsheets and best practices. Larry would stand back, look at all the possible strategies that could benefit his business, and then choose ONE. He didn't worry about whether it was the right one. That is the brilliant thing about focus. You don't have to pick the home run strategy to win the game. Focusing on one strategy means you consistently hit singles and doubles every day, and over time you win.

Focus allows your team to get behind you. There is nothing more demoralizing to a team than a leader who changes focus every six months. Eventually these teams turn in a half-hearted effort, because they know all their hard work will soon be tossed out the door for a new bright and shiny idea.

A good strategy has the opposite effect. It gives your team a chance to work the problem or opportunity long enough to make a real difference. A good strategy clears the way by allowing everyone to say no to distractions that are not true priorities. A good strategy and the discipline to stick to it allows your company to make steady, consistent progress in one direction. It's not rocket science.

A good strategy clears the way by allowing everyone to say no to distractions that are not true priorities.

What makes a good strategy? First, just remember that this is not a do-or-die situation. In small business, we are not putting all of our eggs in one basket and hoping for the best. When Larry decided to begin his focus with website marketing, he wasn't rolling the dice. There were a dozen things he could have focused on that would have improved the business. But he just picked one, and that is what made the difference. Just pick one. Good strategies have some common characteristics:

- A good strategy should take one to two years.

- A good strategy is measurable.

- A good strategy engages the entire team.

A Good Strategy Should Take One to Two Years to Fully Realize

When picking something to focus on, we want to make sure we can work on it long enough to make a difference. Stroke-of-the-pen issues are not good strategies. If you know you need to raise prices, pull out your pen and raise prices. On the other hand, maybe you need to change the way you set prices. That could be a strategy. When Microsoft stopped selling "shrink-wrapped" software and started selling Office 365 as a subscription service, it was a major strategy that took several years to roll out. There may be issues or opportunities that need a few weeks of attention. If that's the case, delegate them to someone or mark out the time on your own calendar to get them done. Save your team for the big stuff. Strategies that will take about two years are ideal.

A Good Strategy Lends Itself to Measurement

Strategies do not have to be as well defined or measurable as goals. When we think of goals, we think of statements that fit into an equation like "From x to y by when." Strategies can be more nuanced; think of them as guard rails that help us define concrete goals. They need not be directly measurable or time bound, but they should lend themselves to measurement.

Honesty is not a strategy. It might be a value, but it does not lend itself to measurement. Customer retention, however, does lend itself to measurement. We can measure how many customers continue to do business with us year after year and aim to improve that measurement.

At the same time, it is not enough for a strategy just to lend itself to measurement. If that were the case, "sales" would be a legitimate strategy. But sales alone don't quite cut it. It is not specific enough to give the team focus. A better strategy might be "Build a professional sales force." We could measure things like best-in-class closing ratio or revenue per salesperson. We also might focus measurements on the recruiting and development of a certain number of salespeople by a certain date.

If you want to focus the team's efforts in a specific direction, you need to have some way to know if they are making any progress. Picking a strategy that lends itself to measurement is the best way to do that.

If you want to focus the team's efforts in a specific direction, you need to have some way to know if they are making any progress. Picking a strategy that lends itself to measurement is the best way to do that.

A Good Strategy Engages the Entire Team

If we want to leverage the effort of the entire team for a sustained period of time, we need a strategy that they can all contribute to. At first, it might seem like the strategy to develop a professional sales force would involve only sales. But that would be shortsighted. Operations can narrow the choices of products and services by eliminating redundant items and scrubbing obsolete products from inventory. Accounting can contribute by simplifying the commission calculation and setting up a new real-time sales dashboard. Customer service can use feedback from lost and canceled accounts to improve products or prices that make us more competitive in the market.

The warehouse team can publish a list of slow-moving items for sales contests and loss-leading discounts.

Given the opportunity, most teams WANT to get involved, and they can be incredibly creative in figuring out how to contribute. Too often, the leader only discusses a sales strategy with the sales department. This robs strategy of all its power and potential. The whole point of strategy is to get the entire team pulling in one direction. For this reason, it is imperative that everyone on the leadership team accept responsibility for making the strategy work.

> *The whole point of strategy is to get the entire team pulling in one direction.*

Grant was a sales manager for one of our clients. Grant's biggest problem was that he didn't see it as his responsibility to contribute to any team-wide strategy. There were always reasons that another department was in a better position to make the strategy work, and excuses about why his group couldn't have an impact. Brainstorming sessions became comical as Grant sat back and either didn't contribute or outright shot down suggestions about things his team could do to make a difference. It took a few years, but Grant was eventually asked to move out of the way. Your company cannot suffer leaders who won't accept responsibility for making strategy work.

How to Develop Strategy

We started this book by talking about values, vision, why, and mission. All of those come from the leader. They are very much top down. Strategy is different. The best strategies are the result of the best ideas, and the best ideas never come from a single person.

They are developed within a group of top performers who challenge, inspire, refine, and prune ideas until only the best ones are left. For this reason, we develop strategy with the team AFTER the leader has articulated values, vision, why, and mission.

There are several ways to do this. One of the most common is to start with SWOT analysis. SWOT stands for strengths, weaknesses, opportunities, and threats. When we do this with clients, we meet with the senior leadership team for anywhere from four to eight hours and we start brainstorming. What are our strengths? What are our weaknesses? What opportunities exist outside our four walls? What threats are coming at us that we need to prepare for? We fill up whiteboards and flip charts. We eliminate redundancy and discern which items have data to back them up and which ones are purely anecdotal. When only the best ideas are left, we pick the top one or two and develop them into strategies. There is always only one primary strategy.

Gap analysis is an alternative to SWOT. In gap analysis, the owners paint a picture of where the company should be three years from now in terms of revenue and profits. Then the team brainstorms what capabilities must exist three years from now for that picture to become reality. That list of capabilities is pruned and refined until the team is able to build a primary and a secondary strategy to get them to the three-year revenue and profit goals.

TIPS FOR DEVELOPING GOOD STRATEGY

- Use a facilitator. As the leader, you need to participate in developing strategy. That means you should not be leading the session. An outsider will avoid getting into the operational weeds and will keep things moving. A good facilitator will also keep any one person from dominating the session, especially you.

- Don't rush it. Taking six to fifteen people out of the business for a day to develop strategy is hard. But if you are committed to doing it, do it right. My preference is to give them nothing else to worry about that day. If you must, give them two hours at the beginning or end of the day to take care of day-to-day business, but make the rest of the day sacred. Don't try to squeeze it into a regular staff meeting.

- The right people. Larger companies of 100 to 150 people can often have a dozen or more team leaders in a strategy session. Smaller companies may only have three or four. A good facilitator will leverage the size of the group to the greatest benefit. You need a good blend of operational expertise to get the best ideas on the board.

- Don't let big groups do the pruning. If your brainstorming group is bigger than six or seven, do the brainstorming in smaller groups. Then let those groups pick out the idea they like best and develop a strategy around it. Later, the core leadership team can further develop any of these strategies that show promise. Or they can go back to the brainstorming list, prune, and develop strategy from that. The larger the group, the harder it is to prune and refine, so don't waste a lot of time. Hand off the pruning and final development to a smaller leadership team.

Executing Strategy

Once you have your primary strategy nailed down (and possibly a secondary strategy), set some goals for the year tied to the strategy. Just one or two goals are needed, and they should be in the format "from x to y by when."

Next, your leadership team needs to decide what their priorities will be for the next ninety days and how they will measure success for those priorities. Andy Grove, Intel's legendary CEO, built a very successful management system around this concept called Objectives and Key Results. Here's an example:

PRIMARY STRATEGY: RETENTION

ONE-YEAR GOAL:

To increase retention from 78 percent to 81 percent by December 31.

SALES MANAGER'S NINETY-DAY PRIORITY (OBJECTIVE):

To accurately measure cross sales on a daily basis (based on the premise that customers who buy more than one product or service from us will stick around longer).

SALES MANAGER'S KEY RESULTS:

- Get accounting to set up an automatic daily sales report email by January 31.

- Audit salesperson self-reported numbers against accounting reports by the first week of February.

- If self-reported numbers are accurate, add cross sales to sales whiteboard by February 15.

- If self-reported numbers are not accurate, work out discrepancies by February 28.

- Begin reporting cross sales at weekly leadership team meeting by March 7.

- Present first thirty-day cross sales improvement report at leadership team meeting by March 31.

The reason that key results are effective at executing strategy is that they provide a mechanism to hold team members accountable. But for this to work, it is imperative that team members check in with each other during a weekly group meeting to report progress on their priorities and key results. Accountability is best done in a team environment where team leads can help one another troubleshoot and overcome obstacles standing in their way.

The Secret Sauce

In this chapter, I have tried to distill what others like Vern Harnish, John Doerr, and Michael Porter have written entire books about. Strategic planning and execution for small business is not easy, but I don't want you to make it more complicated than it is.

The key to good strategic planning is to actually execute what you plan, even if you feel like that planning was pretty terrible. Over time you will get better at it. Plan, then execute and keep executing.

Resist the temptation to plan and execute in equal measure. Put together a plan for the year and then just go at it. Put the blinders on.

The key to good strategic planning is to actually execute what you plan, even if you feel like that planning was pretty terrible.

The worst thing that can happen is that you will learn valuable lessons that put you in an excellent position to plan and execute next year.

The key to good execution is consistency. If you don't show up every week, your team will forget all about the strategic plan. They have plenty of other things to do. You must stay pigheadedly persistent during execution, and you do this by following up with each other every single week. Every ninety days, get your team leaders to set new priorities. Then go back to holding them accountable every single week. Also, allow them to hold you accountable. Pigheaded persistence is the stuff of legends. Never underestimate a person who will stay with a task no matter what.

The key to pigheaded persistence is love, and that is the subject of our next chapter.

CHAPTER 10

Business as Ministry

I had been working with Gary for a couple of years when one of his employees sent me an email out of the blue. It said, "Gary's not going to say anything about this because that's just the kind of guy he is, but you need to ask him to play a recording we made on his phone yesterday." I was intrigued to say the least. At our next meeting I mentioned the recording and Gary pulled out his phone.

There are a few things you need to know about Gary. He cares about his employees. He cares about his customers. And he cares about people. Over the last thirty years he has built a multimillion-dollar roofing company that employs over 150 people. Several years ago, he partnered with a group called No Roof Left Behind to provide two free roofs a year to people in need. Every six months, the company has a contest where the public can submit nominations and vote on a winner. Suppliers chip in with donated materials, and Gary's employees donate their time to install the roof. It has been a great program for the community and for Gary's team.

Back in Gary's office, he played a recording of the phone call he had made to the second-place finisher. These are usually somber calls to thank the person for participating and to wish them well. The second-place finisher was on speaker phone, and I could tell from the recording that Gary's office was full of people. Something was clearly going on that the caller didn't expect. She was remarkably gracious. I heard her say that the family who won the contest needed it more than she did. She seemed genuinely happy for them. When it was Gary's turn to speak, he said, "Well, we've been talking here in the office, and everyone here is behind you. We're going to do your roof, too. We're not going to make a big deal about it, but you deserve it and we would like to do it for you."

People in the office started chiming in and offering their support and congratulations. You could hear the tears over the phone. Gary had made the recording for employees who couldn't be on the call and so that his wife could hear it. There was no press release, no fanfare, no video posted on YouTube or Facebook. No one was asked to donate time, although several did when they heard about the call. Vendors weren't lined up to contribute materials, although some did after hearing Gary's employees retell the story with pride.

But Gary's not alone. Another client, Dean, was walking through his company's parking lot one day and noticed balding tires on a new employee's car. He knew she had just moved from out of state and still had to make a couple of trips back up north to take care of some things before she could move to Florida permanently. He retraced his steps across the parking lot, where a team of mobile mechanics was performing service on the company's fleet vehicles. Between oil changes and inspections, Dean asked them to put four new tires on the employee's car and add it to the bill.

Now, a cynic might say "But these are business owners. They're getting rich and they can afford it! It's the least they can do!" But it doesn't stop with the business owners. Gary's employees were already putting a new roof on a customer's house when they heard his story of stage four cancer and a prognosis of just two months to live. The customer's biggest concern was leaving his family in a good spot, literally insuring they had a roof over their head that didn't leak. Gary's team started making calls. They got Gary onboard, then they enlisted the support of vendors. They took up donations from coworkers and suppliers. Within the span of a week, these employees finished the roof, returned the family's deposit, and tore up their invoice.

Dean's employees had their world rocked when one of their coworkers was diagnosed with terminal cancer. They immediately began donating sick and vacation time so the coworker would keep receiving a paycheck and maintain health care benefits. When this happened, we were in the middle of a strategic plan that would pay out cash bonuses if teams hit their goals for the quarter. Spontaneously, teams voted to forego their bonuses and send the money to the family to help cover living expenses.

These are pretty grand gestures, and we'd like to think that in a similar situation we would do the same thing. But the truth is that for every grand gesture, there are one or two hundred instances where the business changes someone's life in a seemingly small way. It might be a second chance given to an employee, an offer to pray for a customer, taking an extra five minutes with someone after a staff meeting, offering to pay a new vendor up front until things get

For every grand gesture, there are one or two hundred instances where the business changes someone's life in a seemingly small way.

going, or helping employees get their citizenship. These are all real examples that happen every day in our client companies. It is the reason I love serving this group so much.

Why do business owners decide to work for themselves? They may want more control or autonomy. They may see a better way, and believe that no one else will let them pursue it as an employee. They may want greater influence or more power. They may see it as a way to earn more money. But then what?

At some point, the list of "more" runs out. As a general rule, business owners are not selfish people. They make their living serving others. The most successful business owners I have ever met are the best servants. In the beginning, they are concerned with survival just like anyone else. But as growth assures survival, they move into the realm of more. And those things that seemed so attractive—more money and more control and more freedom—cease to be the driving force. It is at this point that "more mission" gets their attention.

Your Business as Ministry

To minister means to attend to the needs of someone. What is business if not attending to the needs of employees and their families, customers, suppliers, vendors, and the community we do business in? Needs are everywhere, and in our society businesses meet a tremendous amount of those needs. To see your business as ministry is to see it rightly. It is also the key to growing your mission and achieving greater things than profits or status.

I believe, and my clients have proven out, that small business, growing with purpose, can change the world in more lasting and meaningful ways than any church program, nonprofit, government institution, social club, volunteer group, or grassroots movement.

Churches need parishioners. Government programs must seek out the disenfranchised or disadvantaged. Nonprofits must hone their focus to a specific group or need that will resonate with a specific community of contributors and volunteers. Service clubs must focus their attention inward at the members as much as outward at the recipients of service.

But a small business has the opportunity to minister and meet needs across this entire spectrum. Its employees, customers, and vendors may never darken the door of a church, but they readily show up to be ministered to on a daily basis. It may employ those at the lowest end of the economic spectrum and provide for their needs while simultaneously employing some who can afford to give generously and abundantly. A small business need not concern itself with definitions of the disadvantaged or disenfranchised to make a difference in the lives of one individual or an entire community. It can tackle causes that may be unpopular with donors or out of fashion with the nonprofit community. It can pour into the lives of its employees knowing that they will transmit that care and ministry to customers.

Small business, growing with purpose, can change the world in more lasting and meaningful ways than any church program, nonprofit, government institution, social club, volunteer group, or grassroots movement.

Who have you been called to minister to? What needs have you been called to meet? My great goal in this book and in my life is to put business owners on firm financial, operational, and strategic footing so that they can pursue their calling and use their business as the very vehicle through which they bring their ministry to the world.

A Word About Charity

When we talk about using a business to do good, most people assume that we mean using profits to support worthy causes. That misses the mark entirely. Being charitable is the minimum requirement for any business. Whether it's supporting the Girl Scouts cookie drive or sending aid to a community devastated by a hurricane, charity is the natural response of people with resources caring for those without them. When businesses ignore charity, it is because they are suppressing this ethical and moral calling to give. It turns out to be shortsighted, because businesses that are capable of suppressing the calling to serve one group (namely people and places in need) can just as easily suppress the calling to serve other groups that matter: their employees, customers, suppliers, and community. These greedy businesses are outdone by their competitors and become irrelevant if they manage to stay in business at all.

So let us assume that charity in business is table stakes. Without it, you will not be in the game long enough to make a difference. But while charity may soothe the conscience of the business owner, it will not change the world. Rather, it delegates the task of difference making to someone else. Charity says, "I will provide the resources while you go figure out the need and how to meet it." I believe our highest calling is to be business owner ministers, not financiers. And ministry in business says something quite different. It says, "I will make it my life's work to meet the needs of others AND I will do it in a way that I never run out of resources AND I will work to meet more needs and expand my ministry over time." Building a mission-driven business should be about the growth of your ministry. The growth in profits is the conduit through which you provide the resources for more mission, for more ministry.

Secular Ministry

Ministry is a loaded term bound up in all kinds of religious presuppositions. But I want to make it clear that ministry in business is more tangible than most people will admit. To see this, you need only to look at some of the most recognizable brands in business today.

The adventure race industry was born from a recognition that lots of normal, marginally-in-shape people need a sense of risk and adventure they don't get to experience in their daily lives. What Tough Mudder, Savage Race, and Spartan Race tapped into was a very real human need. And yes, they contribute charitably to causes such as Wounded Warrior Project. But make no mistake, they are successful because their ministry is successful. Imagine the first time this idea was pitched. "Hey, I've got a business plan I want to run by you. I'm going to take a bunch of building materials and bulldozers and barbed wire out to the middle of nowhere and we're going to build an obstacle course full of mud. Oh, and we're going to charge people $150 for the privilege of being miserable for four hours. Oh, yeah … and our target customer is thirty- to fifty-year-olds who spend their days stuck behind a desk."

Have you been to one of these events? They are often sold out weeks or months in advance. Soccer moms and dads far outnumber college students. There are more love handles than six packs. And everything about these events from spear chucking to running through electric wires carrying 10,000 volts is designed to meet that need for adventure. Is it profitable? Of course it is. Does it change lives? Let me ask it this way: if your company's business was to produce events all over the world that participants would remember for the rest of their lives and that the vast majority would count as a major positive milestone ... do you think you'd be changing more than a few lives?

Weight Watchers ministers to the need for self-esteem. Weight loss factors into the equation, but what makes Weight Watchers stand out after all these years is its focus on accountability and community. What makes people weigh in, in public, when the thing they are most terrified of in the world is someone watching them get on a scale? Could it be that an innate need for self-esteem is being met that is much more powerful than fear of judgment?

Chick-fil-A ministers to our need to experience courtesy and gratitude and the dignity of work. Yes, the chicken sandwiches are good. But the teenagers behind the counter who answer every request with "It's my pleasure" have much more to do with the company's consistent growth and market dominance. And the previously retired dining room attendants refilling lemonade cups and handing out clean place mats are the reason germaphobic moms with toddlers won't go anywhere else.

Home Depot's old tagline "You can do it. We can help." recognizes our need for self-reliance and accomplishment. The aisles are staffed with experts who gave up their trade to come work retail. The guy helping you pick out tile can tell you how to install it because he had his own tile business for twenty years. When you come back later that afternoon the smile on his face says, "I know exactly what happened. Here's how you're going to fix it."

But my favorite example might be UPS. Their brown trucks and the people who drive them meet our need for personal relationship in transactions epitomized by depersonalization. Buyer and seller may never meet one another, may never know a thing about each other, but the fact that I know the UPS driver's name who delivers goods to my customers gives me peace. After all, she knows my name and wants to know how my vacation went last week. I trust her with my stuff, and the person at the other end does the same. She is the figurative glue that holds the transaction together.

I am not saying these companies are perfect. They have their problems and their challenges. But if a multibillion-dollar company can exemplify ministry when it can't possibly know every customer or employee's name, what excuse do we have? Ministry is waiting for you, and when you decide to take it up as your life's work, your employees and customers and everyone touched by your business will be better for it.

> *If a multibillion-dollar company can exemplify ministry when it can't possibly know every customer or employee's name, what excuse do we have?*

Their Biggest Need (and Ours)

If ministry is about meeting needs, I would be remiss if I didn't address what I believe to be the greatest need of them all.

When asked to name the greatest commandment, Jesus said, "Love the Lord your God with all your heart, with all your soul, and with all your mind. This is the great and first commandment. And a second is like it. Love your neighbor as yourself."

I believe that herein lies the fulfillment of our greatest needs. First, our need for a relationship with our God and creator. I have this need. You have it. Our employees have it. Our customers have it. If we ignore it, we miss the fullness that is waiting for us. We look for purpose in places we cannot find it and are left wanting something we cannot quite place our finger on. The sin in our life has broken that relationship with God, no matter how trivial we believe our sin to be or how overshadowed we might think our sin is by a lifetime of good works. We cannot find relationship with an almighty, all-perfect God while we are tainted by any fraction of imperfection.

That relationship with God can only be had through acceptance of the person of Jesus Christ and his sacrifice for us. That is our greatest need, all of us, and if you have been bought into the calling of ministry as meeting others' needs, you cannot ignore our greatest need. I am privileged to work with many business owners who recognize that need and strive to use their business to meet it every day.

Our second greatest need is to love those we encounter. Notice, I did not say **to be** loved by those we encounter. We enjoy **being** loved, but we have a greater need **to** love. Life is full of this truism in pithing sayings like "It is more blessed to give than to receive" and "You always get more than you give." Those who serve, who love the most, are consistently the most happy, the most fulfilled, the most joyful. It is not the act itself. It is the fact that the act scratches an itch deep inside us. This itch is the key to your ministry.

Those who serve, who love the most, are consistently the most happy, the most fulfilled, the most joyful.

What is it that enables a business owner to stick to a plan with dogged persistence? What is it that empowers owners to have tough conversations about accountability and leadership? What enables business owners to sacrifice for years when they could be earning more and doing less if they just worked for someone else? What will make you stand out from other business owners and grow a mission-driven business—a business with purpose, with meaning. It is love of your neighbor. That is the difference.

In the act of loving, you will articulate values that call people to their very best selves. You will lay out a vision worthy of their best effort. Your mission will inspire them to extraordinary action. Love will give you the energy to communicate your vision relentlessly and to hold individuals to the standards laid out in your values. Love will allow you to be the servant leader your employees and customers are proud to follow. It will infuse your standard processes and procedures with life and joy that stand out from your competitors. Love of your neighbor will help you market to and meet the genuine needs of your customers. It will make you accountable for the time you spend and the projects you spend it on. Love will even give you the influence to ask for hard numbers and demand financial stewardship of yourself and your team. Love will give you the insight and wisdom to focus on the strategies that matter while saying no to distraction.

Love of your neighbor will do all these things for you, but only after it does something TO you. It will change you more profoundly than it changes your company or the world around it. If you have not experienced the life-changing love of God in the person of Jesus Christ, start there. Your ministry will be profoundly different if you do.

CONCLUSION

When you started your business, there was an energy and enthusiasm mixed with fear and uncertainty that was exhilarating. And, like me, you doubtless found yourself working harder for yourself than you had for any boss you had worked for in the past. But somewhere that spark got lost amid the weeds of payroll, hiring and firing employees, winning and losing customers, and chasing deadlines that made you late for dinner on a regular basis. The weeds eventually find all of us. To break free of them requires revisiting and rethinking why we do what we do.

Whether you are caught up in the initial exhilaration, fighting the weeds, or just looking for what comes next, it will be a mission that makes the difference. And that mission should be fueled by a desire to meet needs on a grand scale. My charge to you is to grow your mission, not your business. Your business will come. But it is your mission that will change the world, no matter how small or large you define your particular corner of it.

Not long after I started my business, I cut out a picture of a sports car and put it under a clear acrylic mouse pad on my desk. Every

> *My charge to you is to grow your mission, not your business.*

day, I saw that picture. I wasn't obsessed by it. I didn't imagine myself driving it. I just saw it out of the corner of my eye every day. It only took two months before it was in my driveway. That was a powerful lesson for me. I learned that where I put my attention mattered. And if it mattered for something as trivial and materialistic as the kind of car I drove, what did that mean for the kind of person I was? For the kind of business I was creating? For the kind of husband and father I would be?

As a leader, where you put your attention matters. The stakes are higher for you than they are for others. Your influence is greater. Your capacity for changing the world is more immediate. Put your attention on the right things. Start by writing down the values you want your company to aspire to, then put them in a place where you'll see them every day. In doing so, you will begin to kindle your mission. And then you can use the principles in this book to make sure your ministry reaches as many people as possible.

ABOUT JOEY BRANNON AND AXIOM STRATEGIC CONSULTING

Axiom was started by Joey Brannon in 2005 to help small- and medium-sized businesses build and execute strategic plans for growth. About 80 percent of our clients have a second or third generation working in the business. We love working with families to navigate the science of business growth and the art of enhancing family relationships. Most client companies are between $2 million and $30 million in gross revenue.

At Axiom, we become part of our client's leadership team filling the roles of strategist, analyst, troubleshooter, coach, and advisor. Our consultants are versed in accounting, finance, sales, marketing, data analysis, leadership, and operations management. Some consultants will have a specialty in one area or another, but all are capable of speaking to the full range of issues facing the small business owner/operator.

New clients undergo a comprehensive Strategic Assessment during the first four to six weeks of our time together. This allows us to understand the range and extent of issues and opportunities facing the business, as well as the individual personalities we will be working alongside. After the initial Strategic Assessment, clients enter an ongoing, fixed fee, monthly retainer relationship as we facilitate the disciplines of strategic planning and execution on a regular schedule. We work with clients in person and virtually depending on geographic location and client preference.

Our client companies are typically seeking one or more of the following:

1. Renewed business growth after several years of plateaued sales and eroding margins.

2. Manageable growth after periods of rapid change with contingency plans to preserve the gains made in recent years.

3. Succession to next generation of owner/operators within the family.

All of these scenarios are addressed in the course of sound strategic planning and execution. The concepts in this book are meant to lay a solid foundation for this work. If you would like our help with any of the principles covered here, or if you would like to move on to the next stage of strategic planning and execution, please visit **AxiomStrategic.com** or **JoeyBrannon.com** for more information.